CLASSIC CLASHES OF THE
CAROLINA-CLEMSON
FOOTBALL RIVALRY

CLASSIC CLASHES OF THE CAROLINA-CLEMSON FOOTBALL RIVALRY

A STATE OF DISUNION

TRAVIS HANEY & LARRY WILLIAMS

Charleston — London

THE
History
PRESS

Published by The History Press
Charleston, SC 29403
www.historypress.net

Cover photos courtesy of Special Collections, Clemson University Libraries, and of
Clemson University Sports Information Department. Top left Gamecocks photo courtesy
of Paul Collins/Gamecock Central. Top right photo courtesy of Mark Crammer.

First published 2011
Second printing 2011
Third printing 2012

Manufactured in the United States

ISBN 978.1.60949.422.3

Haney, Travis.
Classic clashes of the Carolina-Clemson football rivalry : a state of disunion / Travis Haney
and Larry Williams.
p. cm.
ISBN 978-1-60949-422-3
1. South Carolina Fighting Gamecocks (Football team)--History. 2. University of South
Carolina--Football--History. 3. Clemson Tigers (Football tewam)--History. 4. Clemson
University--Football--History. 5. Sports rivalries--South Carolina--History. I. Williams,
Larry. II. Title.
GV958.S68H36 2011
796.332'6309757--dc23
2011041040

Notice: The information in this book is true and complete to the best of our knowledge. It is
offered without guarantee on the part of the authors or The History Press. The authors and
The History Press disclaim all liability in connection with the use of this book.

For the late Doug Nye and all the other sportswriters whose love of this rivalry fueled descriptions that jumped from the pages of newspapers.

CONTENTS

CONTENTS

CAROLINA FOREWORD

ACH YEAR FOR ONE week in November, it's decision time: Carolina or Clemson. For the other fifty-one weeks, a resident of South Carolina can play it both ways and be a social "state school supporter." But during Carolina-Clemson week, you have to make a decision whether you want to or not. That is just the way it is in South Carolina.

I grew up six miles outside Lamar, South Carolina. A typical small southern town of thirteen hundred residents, it was split about 40 percent Carolina and 60 percent Clemson. And believe it or not, I grew up a Clemson fan. In fact, my family got tickets to the Carolina-Clemson game when the Sigma Nu fraternity borrowed the Orangeburg High School football uniforms and paraded on the field before the actual game, pretending to be Clemson. We were sitting directly over the exit where the fraternity came out. We stood up yelling for the Tigers. Soon, the best hoax in the history of college football ensued, followed by a field-covering fight. Little did I know that a few years later I would be a Carolina student, on the football team and a member of that same fraternity.

I always wanted to stay in state to play football, so I narrowed my options to Carolina or Clemson. At that time, the arrival of coach Paul Dietzel and the options I would have academically at Carolina swayed me to choose the Gamecocks. It was the right decision, and it's been everything I had hoped and more. I never lost to Clemson in my four years at Carolina. Our class enjoyed playing Clemson and had respect for the Tigers. To this day, I have good friends whom we played against in those four games. During my four years, we played the annual clash at Clemson three times, once with the freshman team and two of three with the varsity team. In fact, Frank Howard tried to sell me on going to Clemson since three of the four games would be played there. That's how important it was!

MY SOPHOMORE YEAR WAS really my first true indoctrination into the Carolina-Clemson rivalry. The night before the game, the team stayed in Anderson at the Holiday Inn, and I remember some fans with Gamecocks stickers on their cars staying with us. We were shocked Saturday morning when we saw their cars had windows broken out with bricks. We heard later that it was rumored to be a group of Clemson students. When arriving at the stadium on the team bus, I looked out the window and saw a nice, well-dressed older couple eating lunch. When they realized our affiliation, they threw their box lunch at us and gave us the "Number One" finger. I thought to myself that this game is more than a football game. It's hatred!

I dreaded the game that year, but it had nothing to do with football. It just so happened that my only brother was leaving to go to Vietnam on the Sunday after the game, and I was not ready for that. He had originally been scheduled to leave on Wednesday before the game, but we were able to get the departure date changed so he could at least see the game. I had so many emotions—nervous, scared, lonely—but I couldn't let him, my parents or my teammates know. I wanted everyone around me to feel as if I were fully focused on the game. To me, the game was important because it was the Carolina-Clemson game, but I never would have dreamed that my first varsity Clemson game would have been a second priority to my brother going to Vietnam. But then, on about Thursday, it hit me! This was Carolina-Clemson, and the best going-away present I could give him, and the one he would like the most, was a victory. And we won, 7–3! The game wasn't pretty, but Tyler Hellams, from Greenwood, saved us in the fourth quarter with a seventy-three-yard punt return for a touchdown. I played OK, had some interceptions, and we moved up and down the field but couldn't get a touchdown. For some reason, coach wouldn't kick a field goal. The defense was super! The victory was bittersweet, since it put our time frame closer to my brother's leaving. We came back to Columbia after the game, and on a rainy, cold Sunday afternoon, the family went to the airport to see him off to Vietnam. It was gut wrenching, but he had a Carolina victory to take with him—the best present I could have given him.

In 1969, we won the ACC Championship by beating Wake Forest in Winston-Salem. Clemson's loss to North Carolina contributed to us getting the title the week before we played them, so the annual clash was for state pride and not the title. The game was in Columbia, but I was nervous all week! Our practices were very loose, unusually so, and I was concerned we were not focused. We had an annual senior tackle ceremony featuring a mock-up of a Clemson running back, and Coach Dietzel announced we were going to the Peach Bowl. Everybody was loose, and we played that way, dominating Clemson and winning 27–13, with an ACC title in our pocket and on our way to the Peach Bowl.

IT OCCURRED TO ME early in the week of the Clemson game my senior year that our class had never lost to Clemson and had one more game to shut them out. Honestly, it put a little pressure on us. No one really said much, but you could feel it. We started slowly, and I had three—three!—interceptions in the first half. Fortunately, I rebounded, and so did the team. I threw three touchdown passes in the second half to win 38–32.

South Carolina is a small state with two excellent major state universities. We are in the Southeast, and sports, particularly football, are very important, constituting a major identity factor for both schools' fan bases. It is a very intense rivalry, with the winning team earning bragging rights. Some fans say if you are a loyal supporter of Carolina, you pull for Carolina and whoever is playing Clemson. They say the rivalry is so intense and important to Carolina that you can't pull for Clemson, since what's good for Clemson is bad for Carolina. Who knows?

But I do know this: the rivalry is important to both schools, the state and the fans. For many, it has created hatred, jealously, respect and competitiveness all around one football game. For me, it was an honor and very special to play in four games, representing the University of South Carolina, and never lose to Clemson. Go Cocks!

Tommy Suggs
Columbia, September 2011

CLEMSON FOREWORD

G ROWING UP IN ATLANTA, I wasn't aware of the game that would someday come to mean so much to me. I knew little or nothing about Clemson football, let alone the in-state rivalry the Tigers had with South Carolina. It wasn't until I decided to come to Clemson that I started to notice. Little did I know that for the next five years, the last game of every regular season would give me some of the best memories of my life.

It is difficult to explain everything that those games and that rivalry mean to players, coaches and fans, because everyone experiences it from a different perspective. Here's what it was like from the quarterback position.

In 2001, we went to Columbia to play, and as a red-shirt, I was still pretty naïve about the significance of it. I guess you have to experience it firsthand to really understand. But it didn't take me long to pick up on some things. First of all, Williams-Brice can be a pretty intimidating place. It's big, loud and filled with some rough characters. The fans were so worked up I would have believed they were capable of anything. I wondered why they hated us so much. I didn't like it at all. It was a hostile environment, to say the least, and I secretly felt lucky I didn't have to play.

We lost the game, and afterward, in the locker room, I remember seeing a few seniors from in state fighting back tears. That had an effect on me. It started to make sense to me why this game meant so much. As seniors, and especially for the guys who grew up in South Carolina, you have to live with the outcome of these games forever, and you don't get another shot. I started to realize what this was all about. But I wouldn't fully understand until I experienced it as a player on the field the next year.

THE GAME IN 2002 took on a whole new level of importance to me. I had only been the starting quarterback for a few games at that point, and proving myself to everyone was still in the very front of my mind. The whole week of the South Carolina game is a huge deal on the Clemson campus. Every day, students and teachers wish you luck and tell you how much they want a Clemson win. The mood at practice is different as well. This game simply means more than all the rest. And of course, the media coverage leading up to the game adds to the importance. The feeling from the Gamecocks that year was that we had some good skill players, but their physical play and toughness would wear us down in the end. We took that as an insult. We were reminded of that in the pregame speech given by an unexpected guest. Tommy Lasorda told us, in a way only he could, that there was no bigger insult to an athlete than when your opponent questions your toughness. I think every player took the field that night with something to prove. I know I did.

We ran down the Hill into Death Valley. What an atmosphere! What a privilege it was to play in such an awesome place. I was excited to play in such a big game, and I didn't want to let everybody down. Luckily, I didn't. We were down a touchdown in the fourth quarter, but we drove twice for scores and took the lead. We got the ball with five or six minutes to play and showed who the toughest team was that night. When the whole stadium knew we would run the football, they couldn't stop us. Before I knew it, I was taking a knee to run out the clock. The emotion in the stands and on the field was incredible. The feeling in the locker room was even better. I was happy that we, and especially our seniors, had something to celebrate that night.

The next year we had to go to Columbia. The week leading to that game was typical. They said this year was going to be different because we had to go there, and there was no way we could beat them in Williams-Brice. Normal trash talk, no big deal. But I heard something else that grabbed my attention. Someone told me that the Carolina fans were planning to chant my name in unison while we were on offense to rattle me, so to speak. I don't know if that was really true or not, and at first it was somewhat of a concern. But the more I thought about it, the more it infuriated me. The fact that they thought they could intimidate or throw me off my game in any way struck a nerve. I took it personally. I had absolutely nothing against their players but had quickly formed very strong negative feelings toward the Carolina fan base. I can't say that it motivated me to play better, but after the first quarter I had thrown three touchdown passes and the game was essentially over. I don't remember hearing any chanting. I do remember being a part of something special that night. We had gone into a very hostile environment and absolutely dominated the football game. We could do no wrong and made "63–17" a bit of a catch phrase in some circles. I was officially hooked on this rivalry.

Everyone remembers the next game as the one that turned into the Brawl. I remember that the Carolina players waited at the bottom of the Hill, and that kind of set the tone of the game. We had control of the game from the opening kickoff. In the second half, when we had the game in hand, all hell broke loose as they cleared their bench in frustration. The fight really overshadowed what happened on the field in that game; we played well and won handily. It cost us both a bowl game and definitely added a new chapter to the history of the rivalry.

So we were 3-0 going into the last game in 2005. All I heard about was going 4-0 against Carolina. I knew I had the chance to earn a record for that. I wanted it for myself and for my teammates, but I downplayed it in the media all week. I didn't want it to become a distraction in any way, but I wanted it badly. We all did. Still, we knew we had our work cut out for us. Their new coach, Steve Spurrier, had transformed their football team from the year before. And we had to go back into Columbia to play. We knew things wouldn't be as easy this time around. And they weren't. I played poorly in the first half. I wasn't going to be able to live with myself if I didn't do my part for my team.

We started to get it together in the second half but still trailed into the fourth quarter. Trying to make a comeback, we faced a first and thirty-five in our own territory. I really had my doubts we would win the game at that point. Somehow we converted. We took the lead and then got the ball back with about two minutes to play. We needed to make a first down to be able to run out the clock. On third down, to my surprise, we called a quarterback draw. I was able to keep my feet and get the first down. It was over—4-0. It was one of the best feelings of my life and as much emotion as I have ever shown on the field.

The Clemson-Carolina game means a lot of things to a lot of people. It is hard to put into words how important it is. I can tell you that I did not ever feel hatred toward their players or coaches, but my attitude toward their fans was completely different. I always respected the Carolina players and even now feel connected with them somehow. As for the 4-0 record, I am very proud to be a part of that—not necessarily as some accomplishment that my name might be tied to, and not because of my learned and thorough distaste for Carolina football, but because I love Clemson. I absolutely loved playing there. The tradition, the stadium, the fans and even the uniforms are unequaled. Clemson is special. I am grateful Mike O'Cain wanted me to play there.

I know the joy that was felt by the entire Clemson Nation the nights after those four victories. I also know those were some bad years to be a Gamecock fan.

Charlie Whitehurst
Seattle, August 2011

ACKNOWLEDGEMENTS

M Y FIRST EXPERIENCE WITH the Carolina-Clemson rivalry sure left a lasting impression. It was 2004. Then a twenty-three-year-old reporter for the *Augusta Chronicle*, I was standing on the field at Death Valley when I noticed the Gamecocks and Tigers starting to fight. That was a first for me. Thankfully, I was on the opposite corner of the field from the players. My instincts played tug of war inside me. As a newsman, I thought perhaps I should run toward the fight. As a human, I thought perhaps I should run from it. I wound up standing still and curiously watching what was, of course, a pretty sad moment in a proud history between two excellent schools. What a memory.

A few days later, I was present for the news conference to introduce Steve Spurrier as the Gamecocks' new coach. Years later, I would cover four more games in the rivalry, two Tigers wins and then two Gamecocks wins. I'll consider my total of five games a draw, since no one really won the brawl game.

Paths in life are funny, the way they move and wind and cross. Prior to my time there, Larry Williams had the same role as college sports reporter for the *Augusta Chronicle*. That's how we became friends.

Years later, I was in Atlanta covering the Braves when Larry called me and asked what I thought about returning to South Carolina to cover Spurrier and the Gamecocks for his employer, the *Post and Courier* in Charleston. I started at the paper in April 2007. Spurrier groused about the Confederate flag my first day on the job, and I was off and running for four and a half wonderful years in Columbia. Larry helped bring me back to the state, and for that I'll always be so thankful.

As a part of that, I was able to cover the Gamecocks winning two baseball national championships in 2010 and 2011. What unbelievable experiences and storylines those teams provided, and I'll forever consider them some of my favorites to follow. After the first championship, in July 2010 I started working on a book about the team—even though I did not have a publisher. I fortuitously connected with that publisher, The History Press in Charleston, in December, and we had *Gamecock Glory* on shelves around the Southeast by March 2011.

My first experience as an author could not have been smoother, and I'm still so very thankful to Adam Ferrell and Jessica Berzon for taking that initial shot on me, virtually sight unseen. Together, we all produced something that fans have really enjoyed, something that means a great deal to them. That, in turn, means a great deal to me. I'm eager to jump into the second baseball book as soon as we get this one to the press. I expect it to be out by March 2012.

I'm hopeful, of course, that this football title is met with similar excitement. Carolina and Clemson teams have combined for a history unlike any other rivalry in college sports. From Steve Wadiak to the Sigma Nu prank to Jeff Grantz's big day in 1975, I am so glad I was able to learn more about Carolina's figures and stories in the series. It was an honor to research and write this book. I'm hopeful that we helped bring the stories to life, to splash color into these pages.

This would not have happened without tremendous support from myriad people, but I first have to thank Larry for his patience with me throughout the craziest year of my life. When we signed up to write this book in the spring, we did not exactly envision me covering another College World Series champion—or, in August, my moving halfway across the country to Oklahoma. I kept waiting for Larry to yell at me and tell me to get a move on with the copy, but he continued to be patient to the very end. I suppose being a parent has softened him over the years. But seriously, his friendship—and now book partnership—is very meaningful in the big picture of my life.

We could not have done this without friends who are so much smarter about the history of these schools than we are. Bob Gillespie and everyone at *The State*, we appreciate your assistance. The same goes for the entire staff at the Caroliniana Library on the famed Horseshoe in Columbia. It's a treasure of a building, and the folks inside are even more valuable. If you haven't stopped by Mike Safran's antiques store on Whaley, do yourself a favor. The back half of the building is a Gamecocks museum unlike anything you have ever seen. Mike has passion for the school and its teams, and we really appreciate his help.

Thanks, in particular, to the dozens of former players and coaches who made time to talk with me about the rivalry—even if it took two months for me to track you down (I'm talking about you, Steve Taneyhill). Lunch with Grantz. A nice, long visit in Tommy Suggs's office. Hanging out with living legends Lou Sossamon and Dom Fusci, who played for the Gamecocks in the 1940s. I consider myself fortunate to have fused my life with the lives of those who did and will always mean so much to South Carolina's athletics history. My life is better for having written this book, even if it does not sell a single copy. That's a good feeling, to know you've already come out ahead.

Please enjoy this book. Please enjoy the history. Please enjoy the passion. You all have something special in this state. Carolina and Clemson fans might not always like one another, but they probably respect one another a heck of a lot more than they would care to admit.

—TH

I WAS EIGHT YEARS OLD when my mother, then a nursing student at the University of South Carolina, managed to get me into the 1983 Clemson-Carolina game at Williams-Brice Stadium…without a ticket.

We had no money to buy my way in on the off chance one was available. So we faced a long walk back to Carolina Gardens Apartments if the guy at the gate didn't succumb to my mom's begging. He gave in, and we were celebrating in the concourse beneath the east stands before the game even began. Regardless of what happened that day on the field, we'd already won.

I'll never forget the strange, uncomfortable feeling I had fifteen Novembers later as a twenty-three-year-old sportswriter for the newspaper in High Point, North Carolina. As I covered a sparsely attended basketball game in Statesboro, Georgia, the Gamecocks and Tigers were meeting in Death Valley. The Internet was still in its relative infancy, so I was in the dark until reading about the game the next morning in the Sunday newspaper.

A few months later, I took a job covering college sports for the *Augusta Chronicle*, and everything felt right again as I sat in the Williams-Brice press box for the first meeting between Lou Holtz and Tommy Bowden in 1999.

I grew up pulling for the Gamecocks and went to journalism school there. But emotional attachments deteriorated and ultimately died after I started following this wonderful sport for a living. I have family and friends on both sides of the rivalry who do not understand and might not believe when I tell them I don't care who wins and loses, but it's the unadulterated truth. It sounds clinical and boring, but my allegiance is to calling things as I see them.

Bitterness and rancor between two fan bases is a big part of what makes this rivalry special. Without the nastiness and the smack talk…well, as former Colorado coach Dan Hawkins once said, "Go play intramurals, brother."

That said, I'm convinced now more than ever that the only way to truly appreciate and love this rivalry is to step back from it. It sounds impossible to fans of both sides—actually, it *is* impossible—but the full beauty of it is apparent when you examine it from both sides without the emotional strings attached.

For almost eight years, I have lived in the Clemson area and gained a strong appreciation for the Tigers' side of the rivalry. Tailgating under the trees on Clemson's beautiful campus has become a ritual as my wife and I raise two beautiful daughters. There's definitely something special in these hills.

I'm eternally grateful to Travis Haney for asking me to coauthor this book. It has been by far the most thrilling, fulfilling endeavor of my professional life. I never thought I'd actually look forward to spending hours upon hours combing through old newspapers on microfilm at the Cooper Library on Clemson's campus.

Thank you to the fifty-plus people I interviewed in an attempt to bring these stories back to life. My grandparents, Joe and Lodi Williams, always told me about the Big Thursday games they attended. But I never had much of an appreciation for it until listening to the reflections of people who played in those games. It truly was a majestic event in those days.

Thank you to the people who took the time to scrutinize rough drafts of these chapters: Phil Prince, Charlie Bussey, Henry Eichel, Al Adams, Tim Bourret, Ben Traywick, Johbe King, Trent Allen, Mickey Plyler, Gene Sapakoff, Frank Wooten, Kerry Capps, Bob Gillespie and an assortment of others. Your constructive criticism helped make it better.

Thank you to Clemson's Special Collections staff members for their patience and helpfulness as I sifted through boxes of photos and brittle old copies of the *Tiger*. Thanks to Clemson historian Jerome Reel for allowing me to consult his vast knowledge on the roots of this great rivalry.

Thank you to Bourret and his longtime assistant, Sam Blackman, for allowing me to rummage through all their old files in Clemson's Sports Information Department. Thank you to the folks at The History Press for having the trust to let us take this and run with it.

Thank you to my wife for her great patience and understanding during what was supposed to be our summer vacation.

And thanks to Mom for having the courage to beg her son's way into that game way back in 1983.

—LW

Introduction

POLITICAL FOOTBALL

NOT LONG AFTER HE signed with Clemson in the winter of 1989 as a fast-talking defensive lineman from Columbus, Georgia, Brentson Buckner scanned Clemson's schedule and saw USC as the final opponent. He spent the next few months looking forward to playing…Southern California?

"I'm serious," Buckner said. "I didn't know they called South Carolina 'USC.' It wasn't until I got to Clemson for my freshman year that I realized it was South Carolina."

It didn't take long for Buckner to start living and dying with the rivalry, just like everyone else in the Palmetto State. By November 1992, he was a junior destined for a career in the NFL. Late in the season, he'd made up his mind to skip his senior year and head to the pros. But then he and the Tigers suffered a rare and unbearable home loss to South Carolina, and things changed.

Actually, everything changed.

"I kept on seeing that game in my mind the next week, over and over and over," Buckner said. "So I made the decision over Thanksgiving: 'I've got to go back. I've got to beat South Carolina my last year.' I felt embarrassed."

There are an untold number of similar stories through the 108-game history of this feud, the third-longest continuous rivalry in college football. It grabs its participants—even those from elsewhere—and it doesn't let go.

Todd Ellis, who signed with the Gamecocks in 1985 as a heralded quarterback from Greensboro, North Carolina, was indoctrinated quickly as a freshman in 1986 when he experienced the avalanche of noise at Death Valley. He stuck around and is now the team's radio play-by-play man.

"It is literally another person in their family, that rivalry," he said. "They treat it that way. They're hurt that way. They're joyous that way."

The fire still burns inside Fred Cone, even though he played his last down in the rivalry sixty-one years ago as a star running back for the Tigers. He left Pineapple, Alabama, to attend Clemson in 1947, and he takes losing to the Gamecocks just as hard now as he did then.

Or harder, maybe.

"It really makes my food taste worse," he said. "Back then, we got to the point where we could recognize a Carolina guy on the street without him saying a word. You knew he was a Carolina guy because he had some peculiarity about him. He just looked like a Gamecock, and we hated him just looking at him. Even today, I feel like I can pick out a Gamecock just by the way he acts."

Clemson athletics director Terry Don Phillips spent time at Oklahoma State and remembers the Cowboys' rivalry with Oklahoma as spirited but civil. "It's a lot different in this state," he said. "Here, it's nasty."

THIS FOOTBALL RIVALRY HASN'T been bitter since the start. It's been bitter since *before* the start.

Clemson Agricultural College, which was established in 1889 and formally opened four years later, owed its very existence to frustration and strife with the established school in Columbia. The farmers believed the so-called elites at the University of South Carolina were misusing land grant funds by presenting a sham of an agriculture program. The agrarian interests possessed a sneering, relentless advocate in the form of one Benjamin Ryan Tillman from Edgefield.

Founded as South Carolina College in 1801, the publicly funded school in the state capital was created to improve relations between the Backcountry (Scotch-Irish) and Lowcountry (English, French). More than eighty-five years later, familiar strains of antagonism and distrust were evident as Tillman and the blue-collar farmers feuded with the lawyers and merchants who ran things at the state university. A legislator sympathetic to the status quo was reported to have said that the farmers of South Carolina "need a college education like they need a telegraph to the moon."

Tillman, son of a farmer, began writing agricultural papers stressing that people in South Carolina were being defrauded by the absence of a legitimate scientific and practical education. Ultimately, he called for

Portrait of Benjamin "Pitchfork" Tillman. In 1864, he was stricken with an illness that resulted in the loss of his left eye. *Courtesy of Special Collections, Clemson University Libraries.*

a separate institution for farmers who had been "duped and robbed" by a school that offered nothing more than a classical European education in disguise.

"A natural animosity was there before the fact," said Jerome Reel, Clemson's university historian. "It's almost inherent in the state's geography. There's more to the football antagonism than meets the eye."

By the 1880s, the state of South Carolina had been ravaged by the Civil War and Reconstruction. The circumstances were depressing and disillusioning to an elderly man named Thomas Green Clemson, a Pennsylvania native who had earned distinction as a worldly American politician and statesman before settling in South Carolina at Fort Hill Plantation near Pendleton. Clemson's deceased wife, daughter of former senator and vice president John C. Calhoun, had left him 814 acres of land at the plantation that he came close to selling at one point.

Clemson dreamed of a demoralized, poor state being transformed and energized by engineering and manufacturing. The foundation would be education for young people who were growing up on the farms, and this aligned with Tillman's vision. The two met in the fall of 1886, and Clemson drew up a will that would bequeath his land and his money to the state for an agricultural and mechanical college.

Less than two years later, Clemson passed away at age eighty. Tillman, known as "Pitchfork Ben," helped establish the college before moving on to become governor, a U.S. senator and a controversial figure in national history. The University of South Carolina was downgraded to South Carolina College (SCC) and suffered a sharp decline in enrollment after losing its agriculture school and the federal money that supported it. During his 1890 gubernatorial campaign, Tillman called for SCC's doors to be closed for good.

So there was plenty of bad blood already present when the two schools took up this new, violent sport (Carolina in 1892; Clemson in 1896). The gridiron became an instant battleground for all the hostilities and grudges of people with clashing ideas and passions.

Political football, if you will.

They met on the morning of November 12, 1896, at Columbia's old fairgrounds on Elmwood Avenue. "Foot ball" was a strange endeavor that had been imported from the North, a descendant of rugby that didn't closely resemble what is seen now. The first game, played on Thursday of state fair week, was secondary to the horse racing that drew the interest of the masses, who descended on Columbia from all over the state.

Just two weeks earlier, Clemson had played the first game of its history and was still years from using the "Tigers" nickname. The team was coached by Walter Riggs, an Auburn man who would eventually become president of the military school. The Carolina "Jaguars" were coached by Richard

The 1896 South Carolina College team picture. *Courtesy of the University of South Carolina Archives, South Caroliniana Library.*

Smith Whaley, an attorney who rose to be the state's Speaker of the House of Representatives and a chief justice at the U.S. Court of Claims in Washington, D.C.

The newness and peculiarity of the sport did not discourage some big-game anticipation before the first meeting. Newspapers across the state chronicled it on their front pages. The game attracted two thousand people who paid twenty-five cents per ticket to watch Carolina win 12–6 under light but steady rain.

"It takes the pluck and fortitude and staying power of the Anglo-Saxon to stand up before the rush of a foot ball line," wrote the *News and Courier* of Charleston, "but when Saxon meets Saxon then comes the tug of war. It was Saxon against Saxon to-day—Clemson against South Carolina College—and the result was honorable and creditable to both."

It didn't take long for the game to surpass the horse races as the main event of state fair week. It also didn't take long for tensions to boil over into the first major confrontation between supporters of the two schools. A near-riot after the 1902 game between Clemson's cadets and Carolina's

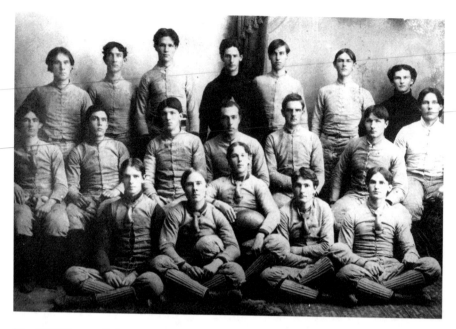

The 1896 Clemson College team picture. *Courtesy of Special Collections, Clemson University Libraries.*

students teetered perilously close to disaster before order was restored. The incident alarmed Carolina's trustees, who already had strong misgivings about the sport's place on a college campus. They banned the game with Clemson for the next seven years, and Carolina even gave up football altogether for the 1906 season.

The series continued uninterrupted after the resumption of hostilities in 1909, pushing through the Great Depression, two world wars, the assassination of President Kennedy and other forms of tumult, both national and local. The 1952 game was endangered when the Southern Conference punished Clemson and Maryland for accepting bowl bids, forbidding the Tigers and Terrapins from playing conference games for one year. The state legislature found a loophole and hastily passed a law requiring the Tigers and Gamecocks to play that year, and the show rolled on.

THE RIVALRY WAS THERE from the beginning, but it took a while for "Big Thursday" to evolve into the October social event that sold out yearly in the 1940s and '50s. Until 1934, when the concrete, seventeen-thousand-seat

Municipal Stadium was constructed at the present site of Williams-Brice Stadium, the game was played inside an old wooden structure called the Pine Bowl. Plenty of tickets were available the night before the game in those days, and often the seats wouldn't be filled until kickoff.

Clemson's "Country Gentlemen" considered Furman their biggest rival before the Second World War—in part because Furman was a power but also because the Tigers had little problem beating the Gamecocks. Priorities changed after a coach named Rex Enright shifted the game firmly in Carolina's favor for a decade-long stretch. Enright, who played for Knute Rockne at Notre Dame before a brief NFL stint with the Green Bay Packers, began his coaching career as an assistant at North Carolina. He moved on to Georgia, serving as head basketball coach and assistant football coach. In 1938, he went to Columbia as athletics director and head football coach. His chief assignment from the trustees: beat Clemson.

Obsession with the game grew in the aftermath of the Second World War. In 1949, Carolina's stadium capacity increased from 17,800 to 34,000, and tickets for Big Thursday were still gone before the start of the season.

A Clemson supporter makes his loyalties known on the trip to Columbia. This photo is believed to be from the 1920s. *Courtesy of Special Collections, Clemson University Libraries.*

Former public address announcer Bill Ouzts called it "Football's Fourth of July." Doug Nye, a longtime newspaper reporter in Columbia, once wrote that it was "a football game, family reunion and fashion show all rolled up into one." It became popular enough outside the state's borders that national publications sent representatives to chronicle it.

In the book *Big Thursday in South Carolina*, Harper Gault captured the spirit of the event:

> *Big Thursday is the day mothers leave their kiddies and trip across the State Fair's dusty midway in high-heel shoes to model new fur coats under a 90-degree sun; merchants close stores; and farmers forget that last bail of hay…It's the state's fall fashion show, unofficial Democratic caucus, annual reunion, and the heaviest drinking bout of the season.*

FRANK HOWARD IS A major figure in the rivalry's history, having served as Clemson's head coach from 1940 to 1969. The Baron of Barlow Bend, Alabama, loved stirring up interest in the game by sparring with Carolina's coaches in the papers, but over time he grew tired of the inequities that came from playing the game in Columbia every year.

Howard eventually got his way with a home-and-home series, and he joyfully kissed Big Thursday goodbye in 1959. Clemson played host to Carolina for the first time a year later, and in 1962 the game moved to the end of the regular season.

Howard, who gave up coaching after thirty years leading the Tigers, said doing away with Big Thursday was the best thing ever to happen to Clemson. Some people, however, still argue it was the worst thing to happen to the game itself.

"I love the game at Clemson, don't get me wrong," said Gary Barnes, who played receiver for the Tigers from 1959 to 1961. "I understand the reasoning Coach Howard used in bringing it here. But to me, there's never been anything like Big Thursday was. Maybe it's because I was a part of the last one there and the first one here. On game day, I just haven't seen anything equal to what Big Thursday was. It's regrettable because it's become more of a normal game."

It is no longer a grand social event, and the biggest knock on the rivalry is that it is just another game outside the state's borders. But inside, it is nasty as ever, all year round. There are few substantial geographic strongholds enjoyed by either school, and the state's major cities have large fan representation on both sides. So die-hards somehow coexist in the same communities, the same neighborhoods, the same offices, the same bars, the same churches—and, quite often, the same families.

"It's a more personal, bitter rivalry between the two families," said Gamecocks defensive coordinator Ellis Johnson, who is from Winnsboro.

There was more riding on it in the 1950s and '60s because neither one of them was usually going to a bowl game—at least one of the two probably wasn't. The loser was done. Here, that was it for 364 days. So beating each other could do more for these programs than anything else that was probably going to happen to them through the year.

The people that support these universities still have that 1950s and '60s mentality. They want to cut each other's throats.

THE GREAT ODDITY TO the fanatical support that fuels both teams is a lack of sustained achievement proportional to the extraordinary passion. Alabama and Auburn pack large stadiums on fall Saturdays, but both programs have decorated traditions. Same with Florida and Florida State, which have combined for five national titles since 1993. Carolina's last and only conference title came in 1969, when the Gamecocks won the ACC. Clemson won a national title in 1981 and owned the ACC from 1978 to 1991, but 2010 marked the Tigers' nineteenth consecutive season without a conference crown.

The two teams were in the Southern Conference together, and then they were charter members of the ACC when the conference formed in 1953. But since the Gamecocks left the ACC in 1971, there have been no conference stakes involved with the game.

These teams are almost never good at the same time; in 108 meetings dating through the Gamecocks' 2010 win in Clemson, the Tigers and Gamecocks have both entered the game ranked just four times (2000, 1988, 1987 and 1979).

Yet they still manage to stuff eighty-thousand-seat stadiums. And in the past, when the games were not regularly offered on television, they'd also fill their respective basketball coliseums to watch the rivalry drama unfold live through a haze of cigarette smoke on huge closed-circuit screens. Not even a combined record of 3-17 was enough to keep a capacity crowd from Death Valley for the 1998 game between Clemson's Tommy West and Carolina's Brad Scott in their last game as head coaches of the respective schools.

For the fans, there's still something about these games that's momentous enough to mark time and dictate peace of mind (or lack of it) for an entire year, depending on the outcome. It's something Brad Edwards, from Fayetteville, North Carolina, noticed immediately when he attended the 1983 game in Columbia on a recruiting visit. The fighting, the yelling and the people out of their seats the entire time left a permanent impression.

"I'd never seen anything like that before, and that's exactly what I told people when I went back home," said Edwards, who played safety for the Gamecocks and later carved out a lengthy NFL career. "I remember telling someone, 'Oh my God. Those people hate each other down there.' It wasn't safe to be wearing anything orange around that stadium. The passion and the intensity were like nothing I'd ever seen. I knew then how important the rivalry was."

"Brother" Bill Oliver witnessed the phenomenon during a four-year stint as a Clemson assistant in the late 1980s. He spent most of his coaching career on both sides of the Alabama-Auburn wars, so he can be considered something of an authority on these matters.

"I've talked to football clinics all over the United States—California, New York, Florida, New Mexico, Oregon," Oliver said by phone from his home on the outskirts of Alexander City, Alabama.

> *Some states—Ohio, Michigan up in there, Texas, maybe Notre Dame—they think they invented football. But all of the places, as far as just pure rivalry, there ain't nothing greater than Alabama and Auburn. People in the state of Alabama have a lot of knowledge about the game just as spectators.*
>
> *Clemson and South Carolina, they're not far from it. And that's a compliment.*

The health of the rivalry has also remained strong despite frequent one-sidedness in favor of Clemson, which owns a 65-39-4 record against Carolina. The Tigers won thirteen of the first seventeen meetings from 1896 to 1919, and the Gamecocks didn't earn their first back-to-back victories in the series until 1920–21. Clemson won seven straight from 1934 to 1940 before Enright embarked on what remains Carolina's only sustained period of dominance in the rivalry. Enright closed his career with a losing record, but he did the job he was hired to do and built a 7-1-1 record over Clemson from 1946 to 1954. Howard then resumed his winning ways by claiming seven of the next nine—including a 27–0 drubbing on the last Big Thursday.

Steve Spurrier and Tommy Bowden watch warm-ups before the 2006 game. *Courtesy of Clemson University Sports Information Department.*

When the Gamecocks concluded an epic 56–20 smashing of Clemson in 1975, Carolina fans thought they'd finally wrested control of the rivalry. But over the next thirty-three years, the Tigers would beat the Gamecocks twenty-four times. Thirteen of those victories were by sixteen points or more. And even when the Tigers descended into mediocrity after the glory days of the 1980s, they still managed to beat Carolina twelve times in sixteen meetings from 1993 to 2008. Tommy Bowden compiled a 7-2 record against the Gamecocks from 1999 to 2007, possibly saving his job with a few of those victories. Steve Spurrier stumbled against the Tigers early, losing three of his first four before turning things around with blowout victories in 2009 and 2010.

Clemson supporters believe more than a century of dominance gives them the right to brag despite the recent shift in the series. And they're still holding out hope that the Gamecocks' run of success is an aberration.

"They're like the Chicago Cubs to me—the lovable losers," said Keith Jennings, who grew up on the rivalry in Summerville before playing tight end for the Tigers from 1985 to 1988. "I hate to bash them, but I don't associate them with winning."

THE RIVALRY HAS ACCUMULATED a long list of stories, both quirky and amusing, complementing the edginess with an ample dose of charm:

- In 1902, Gamecocks coach Bob Williams presided over an uplifting victory over a Clemson team coached by John Heisman. Williams later ended up coaching the Tigers and compiled a 3-1-1 record against the Gamecocks. Between his two stints at Clemson (from 1915 to 1926), Williams practiced law in Roanoke, Virginia, and was the city's mayor.

- In 1915, several Carolina players were exposed as "ringers" who weren't on the roster, didn't attend school and had been paid by alums for their services.

- In 1925, Carolina punter Bill Rogers scored a touchdown on his own kick when it hit the shoulders of a Clemson player and bounced across the field. Rogers recovered the live ball and ran seventeen yards for a 10–0 lead in the Gamecocks' 33–0 victory.

- When Clemson broke a three-game losing streak to the Gamecocks in 1927, some visionary fans came up with an odd idea to tear down the goal posts. Another fan reportedly plucked the feathers from a dead rooster and tied it to the radiator cap of a car.

- In 1928, Clemson wore orange jerseys for the first time. Two-way star O.K. Pressley made the occasion memorable for another reason by shaking off an injury to record tackles for lost yardage on four consecutive plays. It helped turn momentum in Clemson's favor, and the Tigers won 32–0. Soon thereafter, Pressley became the school's first All-American in any sport.

- Cary Cox played on the 1942 Clemson team that beat Carolina, then joined a navy college-training program a year later and ended up in Columbia. He played for the Gamecocks and sparked them to a 33–6 victory, and after the Second World War, he was back at Clemson and faced Carolina as a captain for the 1947 game.

- During the height of Big Thursday, the governor of South Carolina would attend the game and ceremonially switch sides at halftime so as not to create the appearance of partiality.

- In 1943, with Carolina holding a large lead late, a Gamecock entered as a substitute for lineman Dom Fusci. The only way for Fusci to get off the field in time, without incurring a penalty, was to head toward the Clemson sideline. As he exited, he nearly ran head-on into a grumpy Howard. Fusci bragged to Howard about his deceptive speed. Howard responded with a string of obscenities. Before returning to his own sideline, Fusci then polished off a hot dog he bummed from a vendor near the bench. Why? "Because I was hungry," Fusci said, years later.

■ In 1959, a Clemson freshman named Bill Hendrix was seated near the Clemson sideline and saw a live gamecock get loose on Carolina's side. He dashed across the field, scooped up the gamecock and ran back to safety. Hendrix later became chairman of Clemson's board of trustees, and he still has a photograph of the theft that ran in the *Charlotte Observer.* "In today's world I'd be put in the jailhouse," Hendrix said. "But back then you could do things like that. Who'd have thought that a future chairman of the board would steal a chicken?"

■ In 1963, Doug Nye was a young sports editor for the *Sumter Item* newspaper. He coined the term "Chicken Curse" in a column to explain the Gamecocks' seemingly eternal habit of blowing opportunities at the worst possible moment. The article provoked an angry phone call from Carolina coach Marvin Bass, whose team was in the midst of a 1-8-1 season. The Chicken Curse gradually became part of the rivalry's lexicon, and some associated it with Ben Tillman's 1890 condemnation of the state school.

■ Hootie Ingram, Howard's replacement, did away with the Tigers' routine of running down the Hill. Clemson had a 6-9 record in home games after the change, and before the 1972 game against Carolina, the seniors asked Ingram if the tradition could be revived. Ingram assented, and the Tigers beat the Gamecocks 7–6. They've been dashing down the Hill ever since.

■ In 1976, Clemson was a no-show for pre-game warm-ups at Death Valley before the regular-season finale. Coach Red Parker wanted to fire up his team by having a private, full-contact practice on a nearby soccer field. The tactic worked, as the Tigers waxed the Gamecocks 28–9 and denied them a bowl trip. The standout for Clemson that day: freshman defensive back Rex Varn, a grandson of Enright.

■ In 1981, Clemson fans descended on Williams-Brice Stadium with sacks of oranges to celebrate their anticipated trip to the Orange Bowl. Gamecocks authorities didn't realize what was up until thousands of fans were through the turnstiles, and the Tigers' 29–13 victory featured frequent stoppages to clear the hundreds of oranges hurled onto the artificial turf.

■ When the NCAA began investigating Clemson after the Tigers' 1981 national title, Gamecocks fans printed up bumper stickers with a different spin on IPTAY, Clemson's fundraising arm: "It's Probation Time Again, Y'all."

- The week of the 1984 game, Carolina fans published a fake Clemson student newspaper that breathlessly reported coach Danny Ford was leaving for Alabama. An estimated ten thousand copies of the "special edition" were distributed at hotels across the Clemson area.

- Two days before the 1996 game, Gamecocks coach Brad Scott awoke to find large, stenciled Tiger paws in the driveway of his family's Columbia home. His two sons, John and Jeff, spent the morning scrubbing away the prints.

- From 1991 to 1997, the road team won every game in the series, with Clemson holding a 4-3 edge. Five of the seven games were decided by double digits.

- In 2000, Gamecocks graduate assistant Robby Wells was fired after he had dinner with Scott, who'd been fired at Carolina and hired as a Clemson assistant. Wells was accused of sharing information about Carolina's defense.

These stories decorate this wacky, magnetic rivalry. Here are twenty that define it.

1

A NEAR-DEATH EXPERIENCE

1902

CAROLINA AND CLEMSON HAD met a mere five times, and yet it was already perfectly acceptable to call their relationship a storied rivalry as the two prepared to wage another gridiron battle in late October 1902.

It was also accurate to call it a highly anticipated game that happened to be the prime social event during state fair week in downtown Columbia. In fact, a newspaper article even called it "Big Thursday." That designation was still decades from becoming synonymous with the rivalry, but even in 1902 the game was undoubtedly a big deal.

And a day after a determined Gamecocks team finally vanquished its nemesis in a 12–6 triumph, the rivalry came perilously close to perishing in its infancy during a tense, dramatic standoff between armed students of both schools.

The state fair, run by the South Carolina Agricultural and Mechanical Society, was born in the days of Reconstruction and had been in business since 1869. By 1902, the fair and carnival attraction drew people from all over the state who began pouring from trains Sunday night and continued throughout the week.

Band concerts began in the streets at eight thirty in the morning starting Tuesday. In addition to military and carnival bands, an outfit known as Pinckney's Colored Band was enlisted to "whoop 'em up" around the trains and other heavily trafficked areas, according to *The State* newspaper.

Among the major attractions was a high dive stationed at the corner of Main and Blanding Streets. At 4:00 p.m. and 8:30 p.m. each day, a champion high diver and bridge jumper would soar from a perch higher than any building in the city and plunge into a container of water eight feet deep. The famous Bostock's wild animal show featured the "king of beasts," a lion named Wallace. The lion's trainer, a Frenchwoman named Charlotte Pianka, was distinguished "among the greatest female lion subjugators the world has ever known." The sounds and smells of cattle, horses and poultry permeated the atmosphere. The poultry exhibit was said to be the "finest collection of fowls ever exhibited here." The Vaudeville Dog Circus presented dog and pony shows. Downtown would light up every night after 6:00 p.m. with "electric illumination" shows that awed the masses.

HEAVY RAINS DESCENDED EARLY in the week, and the precipitation was viewed as a blessing because it washed away the dust that typically bothered fairgoers. The newspaper ran a special advertisement for a diarrhea remedy that was necessary from "the excitement incident to traveling and change of food and water." Another ad, taking up much of a page, boasted of big bargains on organs that ran from $25 to $100. Arrests were common during fair week, with men drawing assorted convictions, including resisting arrest, carrying corn liquor without a license and "running fake shows." Fines ranged from five cents to $1.

Six years earlier, when Clemson and Carolina played "foot ball" for the first time, the game was an undercard to the horse races. But by 1902, the rivalry occupied center stage. An article in Tuesday's edition of *The State* chronicled pomp and circumstance in its primitive stages:

> *The friends and alumni of the respective colleges flock to the fair grounds on the day of the great game, and the college colors of each institution are very much in evidence on the day of the game. The garnet and black and the purple and orange cause no little comment when seen on the jackets of the fair ones who seem to take as much interest in the game as any one else. The college girl, the society girl—all the girls—turn out in full force on Thursday, and very few are seen without the college colors of one of their rivals.*

Clemson had become a power under coach John Heisman, a University of Pennsylvania graduate who was coaching at Auburn when Walter Riggs lured him to the foothills of South Carolina for a hefty salary of $1,800 a year. Heisman's first season produced an undefeated record and a Southern

John Heisman coached at Clemson from 1900 to 1903. He lifted the team from obscurity to powerhouse status during his short tenure, compiling a 19-3-2 record before leaving for Georgia Tech. *Courtesy of Special Collections, Clemson University Libraries.*

Intercollegiate Athletic Association title, his team clobbering Davidson, Wofford, Carolina, Georgia, Virginia Tech and Alabama by a combined score of 222–10. The Tigers posted a 3-1-1 record in 1901 and were 3-0 heading into the 1902 game in Columbia, having routed Furman and Georgia Tech the previous two weeks.

Heisman had already distinguished himself for creative methods and novel ideas. He was regarded as a master of trickery, and a few years later, he would invent the forward pass after leaving Clemson for Georgia Tech. In the 1902–3 Clemson yearbook, Heisman penned an essay entitled "Football at Clemson" in which he emphasized a

> *greater demand than ever for scientifica and original coaches—coaches who can devise plays that will gain ground in spite of the best and most up-to-date knowledge of the principles of defense.*

At Clemson College we have a style of football play radically different from any other on earth. Its notoriety and the fear and the admiration of it have spread throughout the length and breadth of the entire Southern world of football and even further. There is not a single offensive play used that was ever learned from any other college, nor are the defensive formations any less different than those of other teams.

CAROLINA FANS VIEWED HEISMAN with respect and even fear given his overall record with the Tigers, and also given the ease with which his first team dispatched the Gamecocks in a 51–0 trouncing. The teams did not meet in Heisman's second season, 1901, for reasons that are unclear. Clemson historian Jerome Reel said one possibility was an inability of the two teams to work out an agreeable schedule.

Carolina players and supporters weren't comfortable with domination at the hands of an opponent that was already being classified as an "old rival" by the press. Since a 12–6 Gamecock victory in the inaugural clash in 1896, Clemson had taken four consecutive games by a combined score of 127–6. But Carolina fielded a strong team in 1902, coached by Bob Williams and Christie Benet, and had outscored the opposition 98–0 coming in. The game was viewed as a tossup, in part because Clemson returned just two players from the previous year's varsity squad.

The two teams managed to secure a famous referee named Richard "Bronco" Armstrong to work the game. The Virginia native and Yale graduate was "as familiar with football as a boarding house keeper with ham and eggs," according to *The State*, and his authoritative presence was viewed with relief because the common "wrangling and disputes" over rules would be minimized.

A special train carrying about four hundred cadets, plus faculty and families, was scheduled to leave Clemson late Wednesday afternoon for the five-hour trip to Columbia. A correspondent from Clemson composed an article for Wednesday's front page of *The State* with a Clemson College dateline, describing the scene from the rural school that had opened its doors nine years earlier:

There is much enthusiasm here over this trip. Everybody is expecting a good time…The doubt about the result of the game of football between the South Carolina college and Clemson has caused every man to feel it is his duty to go and cheer the team on to victory if possible. There is no question

*about the fact that it is going to hurt the boys and hurt them bad if they lose
this game to Carolina.*

There was abundant excitement about the trip among cadets in
anticipation of a rare trip to the city, a respite from the strict, regimented
day-to-day existence at the remote school. In Columbia, an air of hospitality
accompanied the imminent arrival of the guests from the upcountry. A story
ran in *The State* six days before the game with the headline: "Coming of
Clemson Cadets…Society will do its part to make stay a pleasant one."

FOOTBALL IN THOSE DAYS only faintly resembled what is seen today. A
touchdown counted as five points. Offenses were given three downs to make
five yards. The forward pass was illegal. Coaches were not allowed to coach
during games, that duty falling to team captains. When Clemson took up
football in 1896, two years after Carolina began playing the sport, the teams
wore laced, leather jackets. There was no headgear and minimal padding.
The squad sizes were small, with few in-game substitutions. Heisman rarely
used more than five reserves, and on occasion the team manager entered the
game in emergency situations.

Football began in the North—the first official match was in 1869
between Rutgers and Princeton—and was thus viewed with skepticism
when it was imported to the South by non-southerners who had witnessed
the growth and popularity generated in large part by Harvard, Yale and
Princeton. The brutality of the sport also drew criticism from academics,
who thought it had no place in a college setting. In 1905, a rash of deaths in
games compelled President Theodore Roosevelt to threaten a banning of
the sport. Yet by this time, the South's growing enchantment with college
athletics in general and football in particular was becoming evident. *The
Oconeean*, Clemson's yearbook, wrote that athletics "not only develops a
man physically, but it also develops him mentally and morally, and causes
him to have a higher sense of honor and integrity, and increases the college
spirit of the whole student body."

What was forecast as a "battle royal" drew an estimated three thousand
people to the fairgrounds on Elmwood Avenue. Two open carriages, one
representing Clemson and the other Carolina, were positioned on each
sideline and filled with women supporting each team. The weather was
unseasonably warm as fans gathered for the 11:00 a.m. kickoff and placed
bets on the score. Richard Smith Whaley, the coach who had presided over

Clemson cadets board the train at the Calhoun depot for the ride to Columbia in the 1910s. *Courtesy of Special Collections, Clemson University Libraries.*

the 1896 victory over Clemson, was present as a spectator. So was Walter Riggs, a professor of mechanical engineering who later would become Clemson's president.

Before the game, Carolina's side chanted, "Heisman's day is at end" and "We'll twist the tiger's tail." The Gamecocks backed up those boasts with a victory that sparked relief and jubilation. A special defensive formation by coach Bob Williams was credited with derailing Heisman's offensive machine.

"Clemson tried every trick play in their catalogue and failed utterly at all of them," *The State* observed. "Carolina started out with her eye on the ball and never lost sight of it from start to finish."

A day later, Heisman would tell the press that Carolina was equal to any team in the South. He also said he believed the interruption of his team's dominance over the Gamecocks was good for the rivalry and would lead to more interest in future games between the two teams.

And then the rivalry almost died.

AFTER THE GAME, JOYOUS Carolina students celebrated downtown by unveiling a large transparency that depicted a Gamecock crowing over a wounded Tiger. Clemson cadets were not amused, and a bloody confrontation followed after they tore down the image. The Carolina side claimed later that cadets brandished swords and wounded two students. The Clemson side claimed later that Carolina students brandished brass knuckles and inflicted injuries.

The account from Charleston's *News and Courier* read:

> *The South Carolina College boys were naturally very happy to-night. They had a great jubilee as the result of their victory over Clemson College. About 9 o'clock there came near being a serious row between the Clemson and Carolina boys. The South Carolina College boys had a large transparency with a tiger representing the Clemson team and a game cock on top of this tiger. The tiger had a twist in its tail. The South Carolina College boys were marching down Main street with the transparency when a body of Clemson boys rushed into the South Carolina College boys' ranks to capture the offending display. It was not ten seconds before a good row was going on. Sticks were in use and the South Carolina boys were incensed because one of the Clemson boys struck one of their number over the head with his drawn sword.*

James Rion McKissic, a future president at Carolina, was involved in the 1902 confrontation between Carolina students and Clemson cadets. *Courtesy of the University of South Carolina Archives, South Caroliniana Library.*

The cadets issued an ultimatum: don't dare bring a similar transparency to the popular Elks parade the next night. Carolina's students did not oblige, redrawing the image on another piece of cloth and displaying it at the parade. The series of events that followed was disputed between the two sides, but it was generally accepted that Clemson's cadets marched to Carolina's campus with swords and bayonets drawn. A vastly outnumbered group of Carolina students, armed with shotguns and pistols, barricaded themselves behind the eight-foot walls that surrounded the Horseshoe. Jerome Reel, the Clemson historian, says the fault was clearly with the cadets. "They were hot-headed and inflamed. The Carolina kids were very proud, and they taunted them. It's the nature of kids. And the reaction was an overreaction: 'Fix bayonets and march.'"

James Rion McKissic, a Carolina sophomore who would later become the school's president, was armed with a handgun. A fellow student told him, "Make every shot count." The two sides were seething and on the verge of a bloody—and, very likely, deadly—riot.

From the mayhem, a peacemaker emerged in Christie Benet, who'd helped coach the Gamecocks to the exhilarating victory a day earlier. He climbed to the top of the wall and offered to fight any cadet to settle the dispute. There were no takers, so Benet climbed down to Clemson's side and tried to arbitrate. A six-person committee was formed with three men from each side. The committee suggested burning the cloth transparency, and Carolina's side reluctantly agreed.

The event did not create much of a splash in the next day's newspaper. A short story with the headline "They've Buried the Hatchet" ran on page eight of *The State*, and it painted a picture of a warm, amicable resolution between the two sides: "Every member of the two committees applied a match to the cause of the trouble. Quickly the flames ate their way into the painted cloth and finally the last shreds fell to the ground in darkness and silence. Three cheers were given by Clemson for Carolina and were returned heartily."

But more details began to surface about the incident, and Carolina students weren't happy to hear that the cadets trumpeted themselves as the victor of the altercation by virtue of the burned image. Benet, who would later become a U.S. senator, wrote a letter to *The State* presenting his account of the episode, and the story gained momentum. An editorial ran in Monday's paper chastising Clemson's cadets while also calling for the retirement of Clemson's commandant of cadets, Lieutenant E.A. Sirmyer, for abetting the "raid" by disappearing after the cadets announced their intentions to march on campus. The editorial credited Benet and the other arbitrators for averting a disaster that "probably" would've resulted in deaths.

"The colleges of the State are not enemies of the other, and they should not be permitted to appear as enemies. Fair rivalry in sports should not provoke bitterness nor should its results breed hatred. Harmony between those who are alike the beneficiaries of the State should be demanded."

The flames were fanned further after Clemson president P.H. Mell wrote a letter to *The State* providing a different account of events while also staunchly defending Sirmyer. *The State* published a lengthy editorial the same day disputing a number of Mell's points, asserting that there was "no excuse" for marching on Carolina's campus and nothing insulting in the transparency.

"One shot fired them would have brought on a battle, and perhaps dozens of the young men for whom South Carolina is providing an education would have fallen in death upon the grass of the campus."

A number of other newspapers across the state joined in the condemnation of Clemson and its commandant. Some historians would later argue that

From the 1909 game between the Gamecocks and Tigers. The two teams did not meet for six seasons after the 1902 incident. *Courtesy of the University of South Carolina Archives, South Caroliniana Library.*

The State's sensationalism made an innocuous confrontation seem much worse than it was. Carolina's trustees later elected to suspend the series, and the Gamecocks and Tigers would not play again until 1909.

But had Clemson's cadets and Carolina's students truly lost their tempers that Friday night after the big game, a budding rivalry might not have simply been put on hold but lost forever.

2

SIGNS OF THE TIMES

1941

THEY WERE HANGING ALL over campus, the signs draped over walkway ledges and flying from dormitory windows.

"Beat Clemson" has and always will be an ingrained catchphrase in the vernacular of South Carolina fans and students, but these signs, made and hung in the days leading up to the 1941 game between the schools, went further. They cut deeper.

"We Ain't Cannibals but We've Got Clemson Stew!"

"Beat Hell Out of Clemson!"

Some were topical, relating to the brewing conflict in Europe—one the United States would ultimately be dragged into. While the fall school semester continued in America, Adolf Hitler's German army was making strides and strikes in Europe that were heard around the globe. That included the Carolina campus, where football and warfare provided the perfect salvo for placards.

"V (for victory) Carolina and England!" another one of the student's signs said.

Then the most pointed: "Roses are red, violets are blue. Down with Hitler and Clemson too!"

It was technically not a sign, but striking a similar chord, the Sigma Nu fraternity had its own take on anti-Tigers symbolism. A mock cemetery was constructed in the courtyard outside the dormitory where the brothers met. Eleven white crosses dotted the space, with the last names of Clemson's eleven starters on them.

All of this is to say that the students at South Carolina were taking this particular game very, very seriously. It was a slow build, the rage. It started in 1934. Clemson defeated the Gamecocks 19–0 in that Big Thursday game. Carolina did not score in the next two meetings, either. By 1941, the Tigers had won seven consecutive times against the Gamecocks. And South Carolina's students were sick of hearing it from their Upstate counterparts, to the point of the signs and spirit around Columbia that week.

"I remember how much it meant to everyone," said Dom Fusci, a native New Yorker who was a freshman at Carolina in 1941 and starred in the following years for the Gamecocks. "We wanted it, bad."

THEY WANTED IT BADLY, too, for coach Rex Enright. Enright arrived at South Carolina in 1938 after, oddly enough, serving as the University of Georgia's basketball coach from 1932 to 1938. He was an assistant football coach for the Bulldogs, and that was enough for him to get a look with the Gamecocks.

Decades and decades later, his players still speak in reverent tones about Enright, whose name is on the building that houses the Carolina Athletics Department's administrators. "He was the best man I ever played for, just a man who you could not help but respect," said Lou Sossamon, a junior center on the 1941 team who went on to play professionally for three years with the New York Yankees. When Enright died in 1960, Sossamon was a pallbearer at his funeral.

The feeling was mutual between Enright and Sossamon, a Gaffney native whose family ran, and still runs, the city's newspaper. In September, a season preview called Sossamon "a little ray of sunshine in the Gamecock line."

"Head Coach Rex Enright, who very seldom waxes eloquent, predicts that Sossamon will go far," *The State* newspaper said in advance of the season. "'He's a great center,' Coach Enright said, and sportswriters of the Carolinas have joined the chorus."

In addition to Sossamon, the Gamecocks were led by Al Grygo, a back who was adept at the forward pass—still something of a rarity in 1941—and Stan Stascia, a tough-nosed back recruited from Enright's hometown of Rockford, Illinois.

Even with some talent, Carolina went into the Clemson game with a 1-1-1 record. The Tigers, meanwhile, were 4-0, and the defending Southern Conference champions were ranked fourteenth in the country. The Carolina students could be amped for the game all they wanted; the Tigers were still overwhelming favorites to beat the Gamecocks on Big Thursday for the eighth consecutive time.

South Carolina's practices leading up to the 1941 game were closed by Enright, but word leaked to the press that the Gamecocks were working specifically on stopping Clemson's forward pass. Tigers star back Walter "Booty" Payne, who played with Sossamon in the 1938 Shrine Bowl, figured to be a handful, too.

Still, some had not given up on the Gamecocks, who did win at North Carolina before being soundly defeated, 34–6, at Georgia and tying Wake Forest at home. On game day, despite Clemson entering as a reported

Gamecocks coach Rex Enright celebrates a Big Thursday triumph with his players. *Courtesy of the University of South Carolina Archives, South Caroliniana Library.*

thirteen-point favorite, *The State*'s Abe Fennell noted a sense of "renewed hope" for the Gamecocks. Fennell said Carolina had "a better chance of winning than in a long time."

"Hope springs eternally in the human breast and those Carolina supporters will be in there cheering for their favorites and hoping for an upset," he wrote, adding that anything could happen in the college landscape by making note of mighty Rice's loss the previous week.

The result made Fennell look like a smart man, and those Carolina students, starved for a victory against their rivals, got what they so fiercely wanted. The Gamecocks rushed out to an 18–0 lead and held on for an 18–14 victory.

There were tense moments, though, for Carolina fans. Down four points, Clemson got the ball at its own forty-yard line with two minutes to play. After four quick plays, the Tigers were set up at the Gamecocks' twenty-three. Two running plays got the ball to the seventeen, but an incomplete pass on fourth down gave the ball back to Carolina.

Clemson had the reputation as a team that started slowly, and the Tigers' hole from which to climb was simply too deep. Five Clemson fumbles, four of which the Gamecocks recovered, signaled the favorite's undoing. Columnist Harry Hampton wrote, "The Gamecocks outrushed, out passed and all the way around outplayed Clemson who roared out of the hills like its Tiger but trotted back like a lamb."

THE GAME STORY WAS on the front page of *The State*'s sports section on October 24, 1941, with the following headline: "Rainbow's End."

"There really is an end to a rainbow and at the end is a pot of gold," Fennell said.

The students understood the riches of the enchanted treasure: they were given that Friday off from classes. That rest particularly benefitted those who had stayed up all night ringing the bell on campus. It was sounded every half hour, again reminding those within earshot that the Gamecocks had finally gotten the Tigers.

At one point, someone trying to sleep got frustrated with the bell and called the police. Officers, though, responded by not responding. They said the bell had been quiet during the majority of the past decade. If ever there were a case for allowing a disturbance of peace, this was it.

The celebration of the victory carried well past the weekend, too. The following month, when the Gamecocks were playing Furman, some of

Carolina's more wealthy boosters presented Enright with a Cadillac. South Carolina was a 4-4-1 team that season, but Enright got a car out of it. If Clemson had picked up those final seventeen yards, perhaps Enright would have still been on foot. He lost his first three meetings with Clemson. Using 1941 as a spark, though, he wound up 8-6-1 in his Carolina career against the Tigers. "The difference between a coffin and a Cadillac is just a few feet of dirt," author and historian Don Barton later said.

Enright's assistants received watches. Winning against Clemson, it seemed, came with bonuses. "Oh, it meant a great deal to us," Sossamon said. "We were really very tired of hearing about Clemson." The unexpected nature of the win, paired with the length since it had last happened, only sweetened the pot.

"It couldn't happen and it did," Burke Davis wrote for the *Charlotte News*. "There was a team that wanted to win for an idolized coach, and that team went out so fiercely determined, with its spirit boiling so hot, that it couldn't be handled. Almost any team would have fallen victim to South Carolina's Gamecocks."

The team seemed to respond to the students' desire to take down Clemson. It undoubtedly had its own, too.

"This got in the blood of the boys," Enright told the *Gamecock*, the student newspaper, after the win. "They knew that they couldn't let the students down when they went on the field."

3

A HOT TICKET

1946

As Big Thursday approached, reports of scalped tickets were giving the governor of South Carolina big headaches.

Two months earlier, before the season, tickets for the game had gone on sale and were quickly snatched up. All eighteen thousand seats at Carolina Stadium were accounted for, as were an additional six thousand temporary seats. An overflow crowd was assured.

Several days before the game, Governor Ransome Williams was informed that two thousand tickets were being sold for prices well beyond the $3 face value. Some, he was told, had been purchased for $20 apiece. (That's $221 in 2011, taking inflation into account.)

Williams reacted by taking the offensive, demanding an end to this "unsavory practice" while vowing that state patrolmen would be placed at the stadium with the express purpose of arresting all scalpers. "This practice, to my mind, will do more to disrupt and discredit the game than any one thing," Williams told reporters.

Williams couldn't have been more wrong about that statement. By the end of the day on Big Thursday, he might've begged for a few gouged tickets to account for the biggest of his headaches.

If this rivalry is distinguished for unpredictable acts, bizarre events and seething strife between the two fan bases, then the 1946 game might serve as the most precise and entertaining microcosm.

THE ANNUAL MEETING BETWEEN the Tigers and Gamecocks was once a supporting act for the state fair, but Big Thursday had grown into a major event by the time the teams were preparing for their forty-fourth meeting.

The end of the Second World War had come a year earlier, and the war had profoundly disrupted everyone's daily life in various ways. No new automobiles were manufactured during the war. Gasoline, clothing and food were rationed through 1946. Americans were united in their efforts to sacrifice and do more with less for the war effort, and people were seeking a return to normal life. The gloom and despair of the Great Depression gave way to optimism, higher employment, an improved economy and the postwar baby boom. Fashion became important after clothing restrictions imposed during wartime, and people felt an urge to look stylish and wear expensive clothes.

Carolina basically became a navy officer-training program during the war. Some of the Gamecocks and Tigers' opponents from 1942 to 1945 were Jacksonville Naval Air Station, 176th Infantry Regiment, Charleston Coast Guard, Georgia Pre-Flight and Pensacola Naval Air Station. The final Associated Press "Top 10" for 1944 included Army, Randolph Field, Navy, Bainbridge Naval Training Station, Iowa Pre-Flight and 4th Air Force.

Both schools experienced a massive influx of returning veterans in large part because of the passage of the GI Bill. Clemson, which once had the largest infantry ROTC unit in the country, was said to have supplied more army officers for the war than any other institutions except West Point and Texas A&M.

The war set in motion Clemson's shift away from the military tradition. The official change to a civilian structure came in 1955, when the corps of cadets was abolished. But respected Clemson historian Wright Bryan argued that the unofficial end came long before, when the board of trustees excused returning veterans from some of the traditional military exercises.

In Columbia, the GI Bill opened the door to higher education for masses of South Carolina veterans who had graduated high school. In *A History of the University of South Carolina*, author Henry Lesesne identified this as a major turning point that "helped further democratize an institution formerly perceived as elitist."

Gamecocks coach Rex Enright joined the war effort after five seasons at South Carolina, becoming a navy lieutenant and coaching the Georgia Pre-Flight team. He returned to Columbia in 1946 and was hoping to reverse his fortunes against Clemson after winning just once in five tries.

A State of Disunion

IN THE FOOTHILLS OF the Palmetto State, fans seemed to be souring on seventh-year coach Frank Howard. Promoted in 1940 after Jess Neely's departure to Rice, Howard won a Southern Conference title his first year and finished 7-2 in his second season. But three consecutive losing campaigns followed, and whatever goodwill Howard had gained with a winning mark in 1945 was squandered when he began 1946 with a 1-3 record that included a 35–12 smacking at Georgia.

Three days before Big Thursday, Clemson's student newspaper ran a letter from Joe Sherman. His job was handling publicity for the school and athletics department, but he didn't offer a particularly sunshiny spin on campus sentiments toward Howard.

"The hue and cry, the veritable din in some quarters—including the student quarters—for Coach Frank Howard's football scalp can not go ignored," Sherman wrote in the *Tiger*. "The war is over; good football players are a dime a dozen; Clemson has a couple of dozen; Clemson people who took it on the football chin during the war with 15 wins, 20 losses, and two ties want to win some football games; in 1946 Clemson has lost three straight; Frank Howard is a lousy coach; the players don't like him; he doesn't give some of the guys a fair chance; he ought to be fired."

Carolina students get ready for the big game by orchestrating the "Tiger Burn" in the 1940s. *Courtesy of the University of South Carolina Archives, South Caroliniana Library.*

Among Clemson supporters, frustration was mounting from the belief that the Tigers' chief competitors were locking up talented players by giving them money and cars. In the *Tiger*, professor Gaston Gage said the student body was too quick in calling for Howard's ouster. "I had rather have a losing football team than to have to pay players as much as Georgia, Carolina and most of the others have."

In *A History of the University of South Carolina*, Lesesne wrote that powerful trustee Sol Blatt instituted a secret football recruiting fund that, in Blatt's words, he could spend "without accounting to anyone, in order to secure good football material." According to Lesesne, Blatt had visions of football greatness—"or at least consistent wins over Clemson."

AFTER THE WAR, BOTH schools began to schedule big-name programs from outside the state as in-state rivalries with smaller schools diminished in part because of those schools' inferior funding for football. Clemson and Carolina also expanded their recruiting focus far beyond the state's borders.

The end of the war brought renewed interest in football overall, and in Columbia unprecedented demand for the Big Thursday game led to an early sellout. Jake Penland, sports columnist for *The State*, called for a bigger stadium that could accommodate all who wanted to see the Gamecocks and Tigers tangle.

"The present stadium at the Fair Grounds was designed for the moment and not for the future," he wrote. "It is an ordinary small-time stadium capable of seating only 18,000 persons…The stadium was an achievement in neither engineering nor consideration of tomorrow. If it were not for the tremendous expense involved, the university would do well to start all over and build a new, modern plant capable of comfortably seating up to 35,000 or 40,000."

The ravenous demand for Clemson-Carolina tickets attracted the interest of two brothers from up north who'd spent some time as soldiers at nearby Fort Jackson. Milton and Irving Rosner sought to cash in on the popularity of the game by printing up counterfeit tickets that were remarkably similar to the real and cherished things.

The brothers enjoyed some success selling them in Charleston before moving on to their main target. They were bouncing around downtown Columbia with suitcases full of fake tickets and pockets full of cash when a printer at the R.L Bryan Company looked closely at one of the tickets and noticed a subtle difference.

Police at the university and city were quickly apprised, and thus began a ninety-minute manhunt that converged on the Five Points business district. At the end of what *The State* called "one of the most widespread and rapidly culminated manhunts in the history of the city," the Rosner brothers were apprehended and arrested. It was stop-the-presses news.

Their bail was set at a staggering sum of $16,000 each, and the Rosners' defense attorney told the court it was "the highest bond ever required in a South Carolina court of law." The solicitor lauded the extraordinary bail amount, noting that "many persons might have been killed at the stadium in fights if the ticket-counterfeiting had not been discovered and stopped."

ON THE DAY OF the game, about 270 fake tickets had been turned in to city police headquarters. Money for the returned ducats was refunded through the large amounts of cash found on the brothers at the time their grand plot was foiled.

The police chief warned fans holding counterfeits not to try getting through the gates at the game. Secret service men, state constables and Carolina school officials planned "a strict check of all tickets at the stadium so that holders of bona fide tickets will not have trouble occupying their seats," according to *The State*.

The stadium filled up early that day, and a seventh-grader named George Bennett was one of the lucky ones who managed to secure a general-admission seat before the onset of chaos. The fire marshal ordered the gates locked after declaring the stadium full, and Bennett has vivid recollections of what unfolded from there.

"They had old wooden gates back in those days," said Bennett, a Columbia native who later was a Clemson cheerleader. "It was one of those that came from both sides and closed in the middle. When everybody realized they

George Bennett, who went on to become a major figure with Clemson's athletics fundraising organization, attended the 1946 game as a child. He was a Tigers cheerleader when he attended Clemson. *Courtesy of Special Collections, Clemson University Libraries.*

weren't going to get in that game, they started pushing the gate. The gate went 'Bam!' And everybody rushed in there. They were lucky somebody didn't get killed that day."

The masses flooded onto the field and had nowhere to go. "The game was getting started, when we noticed hundreds of persons surging into the sidelines," Enright later told the *Greenville News*.

A crowd estimated at five thousand crammed the sidelines the entire game and caused stoppages in play when it surged onto the field. The *Plain-Dealer* newspaper in Cleveland ran this passage in observation of the extraordinary scene:

> *They take their football rather seriously down in South Carolina, too. South Carolina and Clemson did battle on the gridiron at the State Fair in Columbia last Thursday and the celebrated Mr. One Eye Connolly's one eye would have popped in All-American manner had he been there to see 10,000 crash customers employing the old flying wedge and several rougher maneuvers in their successful attack on the guards of the gates.*

Ray Clanton, a sophomore reserve on the 1946 Clemson team, remembers it as "a nightmare."

> *The spectators were on the field and they'd run them off. They were on the bench with us. They were crowded along the sidelines. You just about had to be involved with it to understand. Once all those people got inside, there wasn't room for them except on the edge of the field and in the end zone away from the direction that the offense was traveling.*
>
> *They'd call timeout, and the police would help push people off of one end of the field—and then they'd bulge out on the other end. Whenever the ball changed hands, we had to have a substantial timeout to get room to play. It was a pure mess.*

Dom Fusci, a Carolina player who returned to Columbia in 1946 to complete school after a two-year stint in the Pacific phase of the war, remembers the crowd swallowing players whole if they neared the sideline.

"You tackled someone out of bounds, and you'd knock down a couple of spectators. It was a madhouse."

A State of Disunion

BIG THURSDAY PLAYED HOST to a number of distinguished guests that day, among them Secretary of State James F. Byrnes. Byrnes, who had been named a life trustee at Clemson five years earlier, had a box seat at field level. But the mass of humanity in front of him imposed an almost completely obstructed view of the field, and he spent most of the time catching up with other decorated attendees and was left to follow the action on a radio.

Clanton recalls that coaches had trouble identifying their own players. Howard, who later wrote in his memoir that the 1946 game was the most memorable of his thirty games against the Gamecocks as head coach, wrote that the mob was so large and intrusive that "the Coca Cola guy was selling drinks during the game between me and the sideline."

Halftime kept everyone entertained. Three Clemson fans bolted onto the field with a live rooster and proceeded to rip the feathers off as a group of Gamecocks students jumped from their seats and gave chase.

Jake Penland of *The State* wrote that the rooster was "brutally mauled and killed" in a "cold-blooded massacre." His condemnation of the act later sparked a public squabble with the staff of the *Tiger* in the pages of the two newspapers. The stunt sparked fights among fans, and Bennett can remember whiskey bottles flying.

Bennett might be the most passionate and loyal Clemson fan that exists, yet he's always remembered the orange-clad chicken killer as "a very unthinking, stupid Clemson cadet."

"It was the biggest fight I've ever seen in my life," Bennett remembers.

> *The stands just erupted. It was all-out blood until one of the bands struck up the national anthem.*
>
> *You've got to understand: A lot of these guys had just come back from war. They were trained to kill people. They'd fight you if you just said, "You don't look too good," or if you just looked at them at all. It was not uncommon to go to that game in '46, '47 and '48 and see people just fighting all over the place. That was kind of the sideshow.*

The game was a virtual sideshow on this day, and Carolina ended up scoring two fourth-quarter touchdowns to erase a 14–12 lead the Tigers carried into the fourth quarter.

With a 26–14 victory that initiated his mastery of Howard and Clemson—seven wins, one loss and a tie over the next nine years—Enright was a tired man after returning home from the crazy day at the fairgrounds.

He was scheduled to board a train for New York several hours after the game to scout Duke in its game at Army. But he dozed off, and the Silver Meteor line was close to departure when a faculty member called police and asked if the conquering hero might receive a police escort to the station.

Came the quick reply from the police spokesman, "That man can have anything he wants in Columbia tonight." A motorcycle escort was quickly dispatched to Enright's neighborhood, and the high-speed trip to the train station put the coach inside the doors and in his seat just moments before departure.

The Rosner brothers were on trial soon thereafter. When witnesses were called, one of the many counterfeit victims remarked, "Come on, suckers." The brothers were convicted of forgery and receiving money under false pretenses. They were sentenced with one-way passes to Central Correctional Institution, and these tickets were legitimate.

4

TEMPEST AND A TEACUP

1948

T HE CHAOS AND MADNESS of the 1946 Big Thursday spectacle was still fresh in the minds of everyone two years later. Antagonism and bitterness between the two fan bases were present in various forms, and they went far beyond the fights that broke out all over the stadium at halftime in 1946 after three Clemson fans pranced to midfield and killed a rooster.

Staying in downtown Columbia the night before the game was becoming a pain for Clemson coach Frank Howard, his staff and players. Carolina students had taken to burning a stuffed tiger in effigy outside the hotel and spending most of the night doing anything and everything they could to ensure agitation and sleeplessness on the part of their visitors.

Phil Prince, hero of the 1948 game, remembers the commotion the night before Big Thursday. "They'd lead cheers and yell and bang on things. It was pretty loud. I usually slept through it, but I don't know how many of my teammates did."

The twelve-story Wade Hampton Hotel, across the street from the statehouse, was built in the early 1940s. It was known as the finest hotel in Columbia for a number of years and was a favorite haunt of politicians. It was demolished in the 1980s, and a high-rise office tower now stands on the site.

Fred Cone, sophomore fullback on the 1948 team, said the night-before shenanigans outside the hotel probably helped galvanize the Tigers:

We couldn't go out the night before the game, so we'd look out our windows and see them burning the tiger on the steps of the capitol. That kind of

Running back Fred Cone, pictured when he served as an assistant coach for the Tigers, was the first player in Clemson history to rush for at least two thousand yards in a career. He played for the Tigers from 1948 to 1950 and is in the school's prestigious Ring of Honor. *Courtesy of Special Collections, Clemson University Libraries.*

upset us. And they did something like that every year. One year I went to a baseball game down there, and there was a big crowd of Clemson people. Before the game, they brought out a big milk cow with a big bow around the neck with "Miss Clemson" on it. We were known as the Cow College back then, and anything they could do to aggravate us, they'd do it.

There was so much traffic and noise outside our hotel the night before, we'd really be sweating. They'd be blowing their horns and hollering and carrying on.

IN THOSE DAYS, IT was common for students to raid the opposing campus with designs on covering statues and landmarks with orange or garnet paint. Clemson cadets would shave the heads of captured Gamecock infiltrators and show them off at classes the next day. Carolina students who kidnapped Clemson vandals would shave their heads and make them take turns ringing the bell on the Horseshoe.

In Clemson, a devoted fan named Frank "Gator" Farr traveled from his home in Florida every year to preside over a Gamecock "funeral" that regularly attracted more than one thousand students and townspeople to the campus amphitheater. Since 1930, Farr made the denizens howl with delight by administering last rites and burying "that damn rooster" before the Tigers departed for Columbia.

There was a constant barrage of barbs between the two campus newspapers, the *Tiger* and the *Gamecock*. It was a ritual for the staff of the losing team to eat the editorial page of the rival paper, winner supplying the salt. Jake Penland, the sports columnist at *The State*, was regarded as a Gamecock sympathizer. His regular jabs at Clemson would incite anger among Tigers supporters.

Add to this backdrop the brutal fights between fans that were commonplace during and after the actual games, and a movement began to cultivate a more civil and respectful relationship between the two fan bases.

The Blue Key National Honorary fraternities at each school introduced a "Teacup" that would be presented to the winner of each game. On October 14, 1948, the *Tiger* ran an editorial calling for a more amicable spirit in the rivalry:

> *The blood pressure of the campuses of Clemson and the University of South Carolina are reaching their yearly crest...The relations between the two schools were the best last year seen in many a moon. This was done*

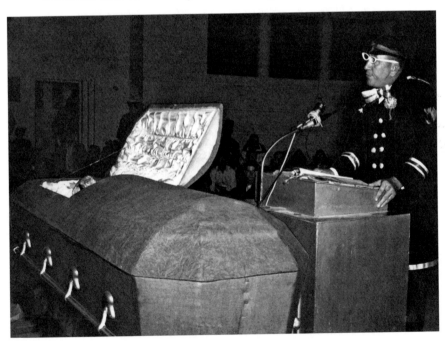

Frank "Gator" Farr presided over the "Funeral of the Gamecock." *Courtesy of Special Collections, Clemson University Libraries.*

through the cooperation of student leaders from both campuses. This year, a similar group from the same organization met to iron out any difficulties that could be a sore thumb for the coming festivities. We think this group is doing a commendable job in closer knitting the students of both schools. There is no reason in the world why eight thousand students cannot come together and watch eleven men settle their differences.

Let Carolina burn the Tigers and let Clemson bury the Gamecocks, but next Wednesday and Thursday, let us again show the people of Columbia that we are "Country Gentlemen" and live up to that standard at all times—at the games, on the streets of Columbia, and on the Carolina campus.

BAD BLOOD AND BRAWLS were not exclusive to Big Thursday in those days. On the Saturday before the 1948 game, an ugly scene unfolded in Atlanta during Georgia Tech's 27–0 win over Auburn when a "300-man battle royal among players and spectators" broke out, according to the Associated Press.

Game officials rushed into the melee of flying fists and feet late in the fourth quarter but could not even slow down the battle which gained in size by the moment. One of the officials then dashed to the Tech band and ordered, "The Star Spangled Banner quick." The band played through two stanzas before patriotism overcame battle ardor, and before peace could be restored to the playing field.

Seven years later, a game between Clemson and Georgia descended into chaos when a brawl involving an estimated one thousand people—coaches, players, fans—covered the field at Clemson. The Tigers and Bulldogs did not meet again until 1962 as a result of the melee.

College football was becoming immensely popular in the years after the Second World War. A crowd of almost eighty-six thousand watched Michigan defeat Northwestern in Ann Arbor five days before Big Thursday 1948. On the same day, forty-eight thousand fans gathered in Knoxville, Tennessee, to witness Tennessee's win over Alabama.

Carolina Stadium, constructed in 1934 as a Works Progress Administration project, wasn't near big enough to meet the demand for Big Thursday in the fifteenth year of the stadium's existence.

Scalping of tickets was commonplace, and in 1946 the sale of thousands of counterfeit tickets created a gate-crashing by an estimated five thousand fans who burst onto the field and had nowhere to go. The day after that game, *The State* called it "The Sardine Bowl."

The stadium offered fewer than eighteen thousand seats, and a bulging crowd of twenty-five thousand was anticipated for the 1948 game. United Press reported that officials were concerned about a recurrence of the 1946 debacle. Carter "Scoop" Latimer, sports columnist at the *Greenville News*, encouraged civility in his column that ran the day before the game: "If you're lucky enough to have a ticket, go to the State's biggest pigskin party and enjoy it. But take it easy, drive slow and play it safe. If you must have a bottle, take the one the milk man left."

Also in the *Greenville News* that week were reports of general-admission tickets in the end zone being scalped for up to twenty dollars. Reserved seats in more desirable locations were demanding significantly more.

THE FORMIDABILITY OF BOTH teams added to the typical intrigue. Howard, whom fans wanted to run out of town just a year earlier, brought in a team ranked fourteenth nationally. The Tigers were 3-0 and coming off an impressive 21–7 win at Mississippi State. A senior triple-threat named Bobby Gage played a key role in the upset of the Bulldogs and another surprising win over NC State, earning the nickname "Rompin' Robert Gage."

After amassing a 29-6-2 record, a Southern Conference title and the program's first bowl appearance from 1938 to 1941, Clemson slipped to three consecutive losing seasons during the war. But the Tigers were on the verge of a breakthrough in 1948.

The Gamecocks had beaten Newberry handily, nipped Furman and gave a spirited battle to national power Tulane in a 14–0 loss. Howard, hoping to secure an early foothold atop the Southern Conference standings, sounded confident a few days before the game in a chat with Latimer: "I believe our team has been in tougher games this season than Carolina and that should help us. However, I know Tulane has a great ball club and Carolina, they tell me, looked powerful against Tulane. I think perhaps Carolina has better players, but I believe we have a better football team."

Since losing nine of eleven meetings with Clemson from 1934 to 1944, Carolina forged a tie in 1945 and beat the Tigers in 1946 and 1947. Rex Enright now had a 3-2 edge against Howard, and there was talk that the Gamecocks coach had been saving some special tricks for this Big Thursday tilt.

Enright told Latimer that a rash of injuries made it hard to offer a conclusive read on this Gamecocks team. The coach put his players through light workouts Monday, Tuesday and Wednesday in hopes that their health would improve.

"We have lots of boys hurt, but they aren't seriously injured—just lots of meddlesome injuries, the kind of minor ailments that keep you uneasy."

THE FAIRGROUNDS HAD UNDERGONE some much-needed improvements, including getting lights and paved roads. *The State* said visitors to Monday's opening of the fair were greeted "by the dazzling glow from the newly-installed neon pylon light fixtures.

"The first visitors marveled at the paved Main Gate and entered the concentration point of the exhibitions, the Steel building, surprised that they were not required to slog knee-deep in sawdust."

This year's fair week brought the return of the Wednesday night freshman game between the Gamecocks and Tigers. Known by some as

Cadets take part in bumper-car rides at the state fair in the 1940s. *Courtesy of Special Collections, Clemson University Libraries.*

"Little Wednesday," the undercard had been shelved after 1941 because of the Second World War. An estimated crowd of fifteen thousand showed up at the stadium to watch the Gamecocks' freshmen claim a 19–7 victory.

Television was in its infancy. It would be another nine months before the first TV station in the Carolinas, Charlotte's WBTV, went on the air—only the thirteenth station in the entire United States. Newsreels, shown as previews in movie theaters, provided the only visuals for fans who weren't lucky enough to be at the game.

On the eve of the main event, Penland documented the national interest this game was drawing. "Sportswriters from the Carolinas, Georgia and as far north as Washington, D.C., along with eight radio stations and newsreel photographers representing Movietone, Paramount and the state theater chain will cover tomorrow's game and give the classic national recognition," Penland wrote.

Penland conducted a poll of ten sports editors of Palmetto State newspapers. Eight of them forecast a Tigers victory, one picked Carolina and one predicted a tie. Of the eight who sided with Clemson, five foresaw the Tigers winning by two touchdowns.

On game day, *The State*'s editorial page basked in the splendor of the occasion:

> *It has often been said that many go to the Clemson-Carolina game to be seen, rather than to see…It is definitely a dress-up affair. And after the game there will be parties galore. It is a great meeting place. And while the score is important—don't be fooled that it isn't—it is definitely a game where the show is as interesting as the game itself. That's why people start months in advance trying to get tickets.*

THE UNDERDOG GAMECOCKS OWNED a 7–0 lead through two quarters. Clemson took advantage of a fumbled punt return deep in Carolina territory late in the third quarter with a touchdown. The extra point missed, and the Gamecocks were up 7–6.

A freshman named Steve Wadiak returned the subsequent kickoff forty-six yards into Clemson territory, and a few runs by Wadiak gave the Gamecocks a first down at the six. Wadiak lost a fumble to give the Tigers new life.

The key play of the game—and probably Clemson's season—came on an attempted Carolina punt from its twenty-eight-yard line with 4:11 remaining in the game. Lined up at left tackle, Prince sliced in to block Bo

Hagan's punt. Oscar Thompson recovered it at the eleven-yard line and barreled to the end zone.

Prince, who later became Clemson's president, had been faking inside and rushing outside on punts all day. On this fateful play, which still seems frozen in time to those who observed it, he faked outside and darted inside…and found his path to Hagan deliciously unimpeded.

Here is how Prince recounts it:

> They were on the left hash mark, so Hagan had the width of the field to his right. I knew he was trying to kick it to his right and get a low trajectory, which would have gone a long way once it hit the ground. I knew he was going to try for the wide side of the field and get as much roll as he could and pin us back in our territory with about four minutes to go. So I faked hard outside and then rushed inside, and Hagan came straight toward me. The ball hit my right arm below my hand.

Twelve days earlier in Starkville, Mississippi, a blocked punt for a touchdown—this one from Tom Salisbury twelve yards from the goal line—was the decisive play in the Tigers' big victory over Mississippi State. Now the Tigers went the same route in a 13–7 win over their rivals.

STUNNED AND DEJECTED GAMECOCK fans walked away from the stadium saying the blocked punt was "a fluke," but Latimer wrote that there was more to it than that in his Saturday column for the *Greenville News*:

> Three orange-jerseyed Tigers were around Thompson as a bodyguard. They didn't dive frantically for the ball, which might have precipitated confusion and in the mix-up the ball could have rebounded crazily for even Carolina to have recovered. They calmly awaited the turn of events. It was a cold and calculating move, methodically engineered, as if Clemson had been waiting for this big chance to concentrate every energy in blocking a punt when it would hurt most—with Carolina's back to the wall.

The Gamecocks never recovered, finishing 3-5 for their first losing season since 1945. Enright was downcast after the game and not in the mood for much analysis beyond this statement: "Clemson has a fine team…that was good in the clutch."

A State of Disunion

The victory burnished Clemson's credentials as a contender. The Tigers, fueled by the passing of Gage and the running of wingback Ray Mathews, went on to finish the regular season 10-0. A 24–23 triumph over Missouri in the Gator Bowl gave the school its first perfect season, and the Tigers were one of just three teams that closed the year with perfect records.

The decade to come would be one of Clemson's finest: sixty-four wins against thirty-two losses, three Atlantic Coast Conference titles and appearances in the Orange, Sugar and Gator Bowls.

Howard, who'd so recently been the target of derision and criticism from his fan base, was named Southern Conference Coach of the Year after winning his first conference title since 1940, his first season.

Several months later, in its summary of the football season, Clemson's yearbook boasted: "UNDEFEATED—UNTIED—UNPARALLELED."

Road victories over ranked Boston College and Wake Forest teams were big for the Tigers that season, but the late-game dramatics in Columbia—and the huge victory that followed—were seared into the memories of all Clemson people who were there that day.

Carolina finished the 1948 season at 3-5 and never managed to win more than seven games over the next decade. But the Gamecocks did compile a 5-0-1 record in the next six Big Thursday games.

Another extraordinary occurrence marked the forty-sixth playing of Big Thursday: a remarkable air of cordiality between the two bitter rivals.

"The sobriety and gentility of the crowd also set a record," read a day-after story on the sports front of *The State*. "There was less drinking and fewer fights than was believed possible as an irreducible minimum for the Fair Week classic."

Penland, a regular antagonist of Clemson who had called Howard a "bum" just a few years earlier, encouraged Gamecocks fans to "get on the bandwagon and pull for the Clemsons in their bid for national glory." Penland also expressed virtual shock that "the entire crowd was peaceable except in some instances. Perhaps the era of rowdyism and wholesale drunkenness at the State Fair game has disappeared."

Or maybe it was merely taking a brief respite.

5

DRAW, WIN OR LOSE

1950

THE 1950 EDITION OF the Carolina-Clemson rivalry ended in one of four ties in the series, but that in no way diminished the relevance of that game because it included one great team and one historic performance.

The Tigers left Columbia conflicted about the 14–14 draw. They twice rallied from a touchdown deficit to pull even in the end, but they finished undefeated in their other nine games that season. Carolina was the only half-blemish on a 9-0-1 schedule, preventing them from an even better finish than tenth in the Associated Press poll. It also would have been Clemson's second perfect season in three years, following up the 11-0 finish in 1948.

South Carolina, meanwhile, won only three of its nine games in 1950, but it at least had one terrific and dynamic player. Carolina coach Rex Enright learned about Steve Wadiak through one-time Gamecock and then Chicago Bear Bill Milner. Milner encouraged Enright, a former Notre Dame back under Knute Rockne, to recruit Wadiak, a Chicago-area product. Enright acquiesced by signing the back, and he was undoubtedly glad he did.

Four uniform numbers have been retired in Carolina's football history: receiver Sterling Sharpe's No. 2, Heisman-winning back George Rogers's No. 38, center Mike Johnson's No. 56 and Wadiak's No. 37.

Wadiak ran for 2,878 yards from 1948 to 1951, leading the Gamecocks in rushing each of his four seasons at Carolina. His life tragically ended soon after his college career was complete. Wadiak died in a single-car accident in Aiken County in March 1952, two months after he was drafted in the third round by the Pittsburgh Steelers and four months after his last game against

Carolina's Steve Wadiak, one of four Carolina players to have his number retired, rushed for 256 of his Southern Conference–record 998 yards in the 14–14 tie in 1950. *Courtesy of Mike Safran.*

Clemson. It was a win. Wadiak's team did not lose to the Tigers after his freshman year.

Wadiak's career against the Tigers got off to a strong enough start. His first carry in the series went for 43 yards. He had rushed for 10 percent of his 420 yards as a freshman on one play, his first time carrying the ball against the despised rival. A Wadiak fumble late in the game, though, sealed Clemson's 13–7 victory in the Big Thursday game.

Wadiak, quickly understanding the magnitude of the rivalry, was crushed. He vowed to never again lose to the Tigers—and he didn't. He rushed for 775 yards in 1949, which included a 27–13 victory against Clemson. Wadiak saved his best for 1950.

EVEN WITH WADIAK, THE Gamecocks entered the 1950 game a decided underdog. Some odds-makers were picking Clemson to win by as many as three touchdowns. The Tigers were 3-0 and had defeated Presbyterian, seventeenth-ranked Missouri and North Carolina State by a combined score of 115–0.

Entering the game, Clemson back Jackie Calvert was third in the country in total offense. Teammate Fred Cone was eighteenth in the nation in rushing in Frank Howard's single-wing offense.

The coverage in *The State* in the week leading up to the game was significantly tilted toward the powerhouse from the Upstate, called "the greatest Clemson team in history" by the paper. "Most observers," one story said, "believe that whatever the Gamecocks do throw against Clemson won't be enough."

South Carolina's victory in 1949 had at least given the Gamecocks a little cachet with analysts. "[Clemson's] high-scoring machine could make the game a lop-sided one," an Associated Press story said the Sunday before the Thursday game. "But past performances indicate the game will be a tight one, regardless of which team wins. The game is a star-maker."

The writer had that part correct, although Del Booth was a bit misguided as to whom that star would be, even on Carolina's sideline. Booth's AP story two days before the game suggested that right halfback Bishop Strickland, a senior who led the team with 510 yards rushing as a freshman in 1947, would outshine Wadiak, the blossoming standout left halfback.

Thirty-five thousand fans were expected for the game at Carolina Stadium, where tickets were going for as much as twenty dollars apiece, an astronomical price tag at the time. *The State*'s Jake Penland boldly called for a Gamecocks upset on the day of the game, "at the risk of ruining a shady reputation."

The tie was viewed as a Carolina win and a Clemson loss, given the way the rest of the season played out. But the Gamecocks didn't exactly walk away completely fulfilled that day.

Carolina controlled the lines of scrimmage on a rainy day in Columbia. Both the Carolina domination and soggy weather were rarities in the first half century of the series. Clemson, though, gritted out touchdowns in the final two minutes of each half to salvage the tie.

The afternoon was a particular grind for Cone, who received a fistful of Gamecock in the first half. At halftime, he received eight stitches outside his lip. No facemasks in those days had its disadvantages, and longtime Clemson fans still talk about Cone's remarkable toughness that day.

"It hurt just a little bit when they were sewing it with no Novocain, but it didn't bother me at all," said Cone, who lay on a bench listening to Howard's speech while being worked on. "Everybody was so into the game and into the rivalry that a little cut here and there didn't bother you."

CONE WAS EXCELLENT, AS usual. Wadiak was even better that day. "The Cadillac," as he was called for his ability to cruise around the field, rushed for a rivalry-record 256 yards on nineteen carries, a 13.5 yards-a-carry average. He had 81 of those yards in the second quarter, which included a 95-yard touchdown drive by the Gamecocks. Wadiak scored both of his team's touchdowns, one a 73-yard run and one a 5-yarder set up by a 65-yard run. "Give the gentleman a slither of daylight," wrote Furman Bisher of the *Atlanta Constitution*, "and he'll take advantage of you."

Wadiak rushed for a Southern Conference–record 998 yards in 1950, clearly aided in a big way by that performance against the Tigers. He broke the league record previously held by North Carolina's Charlie "Choo Choo" Justice.

Clemson's Dick Hendley faced both Justice and Wadiak in his football career, going against Justice in high school and then Wadiak in college. "You'd try to tackle them and they'd just have that move that left you standing there while they went around you," said Hendley, at Clemson from 1946 to 1950. "The moves they had, I always compared them. They were the same type. They weren't fast. They didn't have the speed. But they just had the instinct of how to make a move to get around you—and the strength to run through you."

Carolina did not even complete a pass in the game. Clemson had just four completions. The game, played in what the newspaper called "droves" of rain, was all about the physicality of the two backs, Cone and Wadiak. Down 14–7 in the final few minutes, Howard, recognizing what sort of season it could be, begged his players for one final scoring drive. He told the Tigers the ball was going to Cone on every play. "We got in the huddle and told everybody, 'Now, if anybody misses a block, after the game we're going to kick your butt,'" Hendley said.

Cone, typically stoic, spoke up in that huddle. "Give me the ball," he told his teammates. "If you'll block for me, I'll score." Hendley said, "It was like setting off a bomb." Cone ripped off runs right and left. His nose and mouth bloody from that hit in the first half, the stitches coming undone, Cone scored the touchdown that ultimately allowed Clemson to tie the game.

Both teams and their fans left the stadium wet and exhausted. If ever a draw fit in the series, it was the 1950 game.

6

ENDING THE JINX

1955

S IX DAYS BEFORE BIG Thursday, Clemson's students had assembled for lunch on Friday afternoon in the mess hall when a voice boomed through the public-address speakers, "Are we going to beat Carolina?"

The students were prompt, unanimous and emphatic in their response. "Hell yes!" came the scream.

Trips to Columbia had become something close to hell for the Tigers in recent years, and everyone in Clemson was plenty eager to restore what they believed to be the natural order of the rivalry.

The previous season, Carolina had been aided by a controversial call by the officials to hold the Tigers off in a 13–8 victory. It was the Gamecocks' fourth consecutive Big Thursday triumph, and Frank Howard had won just once in his previous ten trips to Columbia.

This was an unsettling and unacceptable trend for Clemson fans, who were accustomed to the inverse. From 1896 to 1944, the Tigers compiled a 28-13-1 record in the series. Included was a seven-game winning streak from 1934 to 1940, a binge that remains the longest in the history of the rivalry.

MINUTES AFTER SEALING THE 1954 victory—Carolina's first four-game winning streak in the series—Gamecocks veterans spoke confident and cocky words in the pages of *The State* newspaper.

"That's four straight," yelled co-captain Bill Wohrman.

"They've never beaten old Harry," piped senior tackle Harry Lovell.

"They ain't beat me either," crowed senior center Leon Cunningham.

Gamecocks coach Rex Enright was making his living by orchestrating a regular slaying of the Tigers, having compiled a 7-1-1 record since his return from the navy in 1946. When Enright was hired, the expectation from trustees was that he beat Clemson with regularity while merely maintaining respectability against everyone else. When he gave up coaching later in the year, his overall record stood at 64-69-7.

A sportswriter from Orangeburg wrote, "The Birds of Enright can always rise to dizzying heights whenever the team they're playing is called 'Clemson.'"

Yet there were signs, even in 1953 and 1954, that Clemson was accumulating momentum for a turnaround. The signing class of 1953 was heralded as perhaps the best in school history, and one of those players was a charismatic kid from North Carolina named Charlie Bussey.

Bussey was born in his grandmother's house in Woodruff, South Carolina. His father had coached high school football in Abbeville and counted among his pupils former Clemson greats Charlie Timmons and Bob Sharpe. But the family moved to Henderson, North Carolina, before Bussey was five, and he never had much of an affinity for the rivalry before he arrived at Clemson.

"Within the team, there are other rivalries," Bussey said. "I would've rather beat a North Carolina team just as soon as Carolina, because I was raised forty miles from Duke, North Carolina, Wake Forest and NC State. The fans make it a bigger rivalry than it would be normally. I mean nowadays—gosh dog. It hurts me worse now to get beat by Carolina than it would have back then. It's certainly a big rivalry for the players. But when you become a fan, it takes on a new scope."

OFFENSES IN COLLEGE FOOTBALL had shifted to the newfangled "T" formation that was supposed to create more opportunities for explosive plays, but Howard held on to the single wing longer than most. He finally scrapped the relic in 1953 and recruited players for the T. He later acknowledged one of the main reasons for the shift was Carolina's defense scoring all three touchdowns against Clemson's single wing in a 20–0 Gamecocks victory in 1951.

Bussey remembers a buzz percolating among a class that also included a dazzling running back from Columbia named Joel Wells, who later was regarded as the best Clemson running back since Banks McFadden.

"The first year of the ACC was 1953, and we were all recruited for the T formation," Bussey said. "And we were pretty dog-gone good. We pledged in 1953 as freshmen that four years later we were going to win the conference and go to the Orange Bowl. We agreed that we'd pay the price to get there. We sensed something special in the making."

Bussey was enchanted by the military lifestyle when he took a recruiting visit to Clemson in 1953. Back then, daily life for cadets at Clemson closely resembled life at West Point and Annapolis—marching in formation to meals, Thursday afternoon drill at Bowman Field and strict inspections on Saturday mornings.

Bussey fell in love with the place when he took his first look at the one-inch openings in the floors of the barracks, the high ceilings and the regimented schedule.

Back then, few students had cars. On weekends, it was common to see long lines of cadets in front of Sikes Hall (then a library) in uniform with their thumbs outstretched seeking rides to find dates at nearby campuses in Greenville, Anderson and even across the border to a women's school in Gainesville, Georgia.

Clemson made military optional in 1955, facilitating the inclusion of women, but Bussey continued on the military track and later became an air force pilot.

"Football players from that era, when you talk to them today, they either loved the military or hated it," Bussey said. "But they loved Clemson. There weren't but four thousand students, so you had that closeness and you got to know everybody. They have camaraderie today, but it's a different camaraderie. We were close because we suffered together through academics, military and very tough football practices."

IN THE OFFICES OF Clemson's student newspaper, the *Tiger*, high hopes accompanied the 1955 season. In early January, sportswriter Lewis Cromer penned early predictions and had this to say about Big Thursday: "October—The Howardmen put the skids under Carolina for the first time in many moons and appear destined for great things."

Even Howard, not typically known for bubbly forecasts, seemed optimistic as he prepared for his sixteenth season as head coach. He acknowledged that the transition to a new offense over three seasons "has been rather rough," but he believed the Tigers were ready to take off with the T.

"I think we are going to have a much better football team next year," he was quoted as saying. "We played a lot of sophomores last year. They gained a lot of experience. Next fall, the team is going to look like it knows what it's doing—it will."

Clemson began the season with a 3-0 record that included a 26–7 smashing of Georgia on the Tigers' home field. The fourth game was at Rice, which pulled off a 21–7 upset of the sixteenth-ranked Tigers. The Owls were coached by a familiar face, former Clemson coaching great Jess Neely.

The loss wasn't the only bad news from Clemson's long jaunt to Houston. Veteran quarterback Don King suffered a knee injury, and his status was looking doubtful for the big game in Columbia twelve days later.

Carolina had not lived up to expectations in 1955. The Gamecocks' only victories were over Wofford and Furman, and they were not particularly impressive in either win. Wake Forest and Navy had beaten Carolina handily.

Clemson was anointed as the favorite in this clash, yet favored status had done little to help the Tigers in previous years. They were supposed to win by a touchdown in 1950 and ended up settling for a 14–14 tie; they were a decided favorite in 1951 but were drubbed 20–0; the Gamecocks were rebuilding in 1952 but still managed a 6–0 win over a more experienced Clemson team.

The Gamecocks were viewed as the better team heading into their 1953 and 1954 victories, so as the 1955 game approached they bristled at suggestions of supernatural assistance in their rare prolonged dominance of the Tigers. A sign in their locker room read, "Hard blocking and tackling, not jinxes, win football games."

Bussey had elevated to the varsity team in 1954, but King had firm control of the quarterback position that season as a junior. King missed some games to injury, though, allowing Bussey to gain some crucial experience.

JAKE PENLAND, THE COLUMBIA sports columnist that Clemson fans loved to hate, ventured to the foothills the week before the game to get a feel for this Tigers football team.

"Up at Clemson, the Tigers are quietly confident they'll take the South Carolina Gamecocks this year," Penland wrote.

No, they're not in the least bit cocky, but they all admit to having "that feeling" that this is the year for them. And they think they can win even if Don King, their inspirational leader and quarterback, is unable to play because of a knee injury. They have faith in Charlie Bussey, a business-like quarterback from Henderson, N.C. He showed he can direct the first team when he led the Tigers on a 97-yard sustained march for a touchdown through Rice's powerful Southwest Conference Owls a Saturday ago.

And Bussey likes the challenge of being the No. 1 quarterback against the Gamecocks, who will be trying to extend their mastery over the Tigers to five straight years.

Penland interviewed Bussey, who seemed confident in the Tigers' chances.

I like being the No. 1 quarterback for Carolina, and for all the time. I hope Don will be okay, but I hope we won't need him. Yes, I'd rather play quarterback against them, unless it would be against Wake Forest which is only 25 miles from home…I believe we'll do all right against Carolina. The spirit is good—we might have gained from losing to Rice. It could have been a blessing in disguise. And I believe every boy on the team will give it everything he's got next week.

I don't look to beating Carolina any more than any other team. But since they are our biggest rivals, it'd be nice to beat them.

Penland also chatted up senior fullback Billy O'Dell, who felt good about ending the hex. "I think the boys have more desire to win than in the four years I've been at Clemson. They work together better than in the past…I also think the law of averages is bound to catch up with Carolina."

Senior end Walt Laraway's sentiments about the game bordered on brash, given the garnet-tinged tenor of the rivalry over the previous decade:

I actually think we're going to take 'em this year for the first time…I don't think Don King's being hurt is anything to get excited about. The boys will play for Bussey. Our timing is all right with Bussey in there. The rest of the players are not doing a whole lot of talking this year, like they did last year, but they all believe that we are going to beat Carolina. In fact, that's the feeling of the entire student body.

King, whose knee injury had improved to the point that he was considered likely to play, said it was the Tigers' "best chance since I've been here."

The Gamecocks weren't short on bluster or confidence. Halfback Mike Caskey told Penland he hoped King would play "because if we win I don't want them to have any excuses. I'd rather beat Duke or Maryland or North

Charlie Bussey (left) and Don King. Both played quarterback for the Tigers in 1955, and coach Frank Howard fretted over which one to play in the days and hours leading up to Big Thursday. *Courtesy of Clemson University Sports Information Department.*

Carolina because we've been beating Clemson and not those other teams, but they put so much pressure on this Clemson game that I figure we've got to win."

Said tackle Hugh Merck, "The best Clemson team I played against was the 1950 team, which had to come from behind near the end to tie us. I don't think they are any better this year. If we're right, I won't worry about Clemson collectively or individually."

DESPITE EFFORTS IN PREVIOUS years to impose more civil and cordial relations on the two fan bases, the antagonism continued. Early Tuesday morning, just two days before the big game, a group of Clemson fans quietly slipped onto Carolina's campus and painted derisive slogans on buildings and walls. They even managed to vandalize the press box at the nearby stadium.

At the entrance of the intramural gym on the corner of Sumter and Greene Streets, the Clemson supporters painted "Beat Carolina" and "Give'm Hell Clemson."

Jim Anderson, sports columnist for the *Greenville News*, included the following passage in a dispatch from Columbia:

> *And there was a kidnapping. A mock Tiger up three stories on the McBryde Dormitory disappeared. University students were going to burn it tonight. They had to hastily build a new tiger.*
>
> *Officers in West Columbia stopped a car last night and found the mock tiger inside. The kidnappers evidently were on their way to Oconee County. No charges were brought, however. Evidently the policemen weren't Carolina men. Occupants of the car were allowed to continue on their way. Yes, this is the time of year Columbia becomes a crazy, mixed-up place. It's the eve of Big Thursday.*

Later, several days after the game, Clemson's student body president would write to the student newspaper and admonish the vandalism that "left a smudge on Clemson's fine record."

"Vandalism, although it served as an emotional vent for some, had no part in bringing about a victory on the field," wrote Jim Humphries. "Instead, it brought considerable embarrassment to Clemson."

Howard was typically frazzled emotionally before games, and his basket-case state intensified during Carolina week. Tired of all the distractions that came with lodging in downtown Columbia—and searching for something, anything, to turn the rivalry back in Clemson's favor—he made the decision to stay in Batesburg the night before the game. The location was a closely guarded secret.

Howard was so wound up before big games that he sometimes agonized over whether to kick or receive should his team win the toss. Bussey said his coach came close to starting King against Carolina at the last minute, even though Bussey spent a week practicing with the first team.

A young assistant coach named Bill McLellan, who, sixteen years later, would become Clemson's athletics director, convinced Howard to stick with Bussey. "Coach Howard was dying," Bussey recalled, "because he always wanted to go with his number one guy no matter how much confidence he had in number two."

Whitey Jordan, a Florence native who played receiver from 1955 to 1957 and also served as an assistant for the Tigers. *Courtesy of Clemson University Sports Information Department.*

Howard seemed uneasy the day before the game when he spoke with a *Sports Illustrated* writer who was in town to chronicle the Big Thursday spectacle. "This used to be just another game," he said. "We used to beat them and go on about our business, but it's sure turned around now."

The decision to go with Bussey—not to mention the move to stay outside the city Wednesday night—ended up looking brilliant. Bussey played a major role in building a 21–0 third-quarter lead, and the Tigers held on to win 28–14.

Clemson struck early on its second possession, Bussey hitting Willie Smith for a fifty-five-yard strike. The second touchdown also came in the first quarter, and it was aided by a new play the Tigers concocted after watching Oklahoma twelve days earlier.

While waiting for their night game against Rice in Houston, the Tigers watched Oklahoma play Texas on TV in the afternoon. The Sooners

Coach Frank Howard is hoisted after a big win during his tenure at Clemson, possibly on Big Thursday. *Courtesy of Special Collections, Clemson University Libraries.*

enjoyed immense success with a counter play that used star running back Tommy McDonald off one tackle after faking a handoff off the other tackle.

Howard liked what he saw, and the Tigers installed "Carolina Special" for Big Thursday. "They told me not to run it until we got inside the thirty-yard line," Bussey recalled. "They told me it was good for thirty yards because nobody had seen it."

Bussey couldn't wait that long. With the Tigers facing third down near midfield, he called the play that faked to Jim Coleman over left tackle before handing it to Wells for a run off right tackle. Wells ripped off a huge run all the way to the three.

"CAROLINA SPECIAL" HELPED DELIVER a triumph that was especially sweet to Bussey, who also had an interception on defense to thwart an early Gamecocks foray into Clemson territory. King ended up playing, but it was Bussey who drew the raves from the horde of ink-stained scribes who attended the game.

Smith Barrier, columnist from the *Daily News* of Greensboro, North Carolina, said Bussey was "the Big Tiger on this Big Thursday."

"Bussey put the buzz on the Gamecocks in a hurry, and his name was on every lip for the remainder of this beautiful football day."

Enright, Clemson's biggest coaching nemesis, retired after the season and became athletics director. The luck even started going the Tigers' way in 1956, when a Gamecocks fumble near Clemson's goal line—recovered by Bussey—allowed the Tigers to make it two in a row.

Clemson ended up beating the Gamecocks seven times in nine years, claiming three ACC titles and reaching the Orange and Sugar Bowls. The headline on *The State*'s sports front the morning of October 21, 1955, read, "Tigers break Carolina jinx."

7

HOWARD'S SUNBURNED HEAD

1958

FRANK HOWARD WAS FEELING quite confident in his team entering the 1958 Big Thursday game—and for good reason.

The Tigers were 4-0 and had won ten of their past eleven games going back to the previous season. They were ranked tenth in the country. Howard had won his 100th game a month earlier.

Adding to the sentiment, Clemson had taken the past three games in the Carolina series. The Gamecocks had not even scored a point against Howard and the Tigers since coach Warren Giese arrived in 1956, falling 7–0 that season and 13–0 in 1957.

Including Howard, no one expected much to change in 1958. An Associated Press story the week of the game pitted the teams as the tortoise against the hare. It called Clemson a "razzle-dazzle undefeated team," and twice-defeated Carolina was "slow-moving."

The plodding Gamecocks offense was so mechanically boring that a reporter said the previous week in Chapel Hill, the site of a 6–0 South Carolina victory, that "it was the only good sleep I got all week." Not surprisingly, *The State*'s half dozen writers all picked Clemson to win the game. One of them wrote, "Last year I picked South Carolina. 'Nuff said."

At 2-2, and despite the aura surrounding the opposition, Giese had not given up on his Carolina team. "We still have the makings of an excellent season," he said, jabbing some at Clemson in the weeks leading up to the game, even considering his teams' struggles against the Tigers.

In doing so, Giese drew out Howard. The sometimes-grumpy Clemson fixture said that week, "If ol' Geezie ever scores on me, I'll tip my hat to him."

GOOD TO HIS WORD, Howard did tip his cap to Giese and the Carolina sideline. Then he did it again. And again and again.

By the end of a shocking afternoon, a 26–6 Gamecocks victory, Howard joked that he doffed his hat so many times that his bald head became sunburned. It seemed to even those on the field that Clemson might have taken Carolina far too lightly. "That game was won in last week's practice, or rather, after practice," Gamecocks senior captain King Dixon told *The State.*

> *We read in the paper that Clemson was taking it easy in practice. Well, I can tell you fellows now, we weren't taking things easy. We worked, worked and worked. Then after practice we had wind sprints on top of wind sprints. It was condition that won that ball game. We didn't tire and they did.*
>
> *I hated those sprints last week, but now, man, they were terrific today.*

Emotion played a part in the preparation, as well. Alex Hawkins, Dixon's fellow captain and backfield mate, made a stirring speech as the game approached. He vowed to improve his play for the final half of his final college season.

Dixon and Hawkins were vital in the second half of a game that was deadlocked at six at intermission. Both teams had seven first downs. Carolina had 110 yards to Clemson's 94. The Gamecocks' opening possession of the second half set the standard for the final two quarters. Dixon fielded the kick at the ten and nearly returned it to midfield. It required fourteen consecutive running plays for the methodical Gamecocks to cover the other half of the field and reach the end zone. Four players carried the load on those fourteen plays: quarterback Bobby Bunch ran six times, John Saunders four, Hawkins three and Dixon one. It was slow, but it was effective. Hawkins added a two-point conversion, and Carolina was

Coin toss in an early 1950s Big Thursday game. *Courtesy of Clemson University Sports Information Department.*

on its way. "From then the spirited Gamecocks tore the Tigers apart," *The State*'s report said.

Clemson's fading chances were dealt a final blow when quarterback Harvey White, who went on to be a second-team All-ACC selection that season, left the game with an injury. Dixon and White both lowered their shoulders and collided. White missed a large chunk of the fourth quarter as a result.

WITH THE GAME IN hand, Carolina's players began to politick on the sideline to get Hawkins a touchdown against the Tigers. The team had that much respect for Hawkins, who went on to a successful NFL career as a special teams player. "He's the most unforgettable character I've ever met in my life," said Dixon, the Laurens, South Carolina native who was later Carolina's athletics director from 1988 to 1992. "Alex is a West-by-God-Virginian. He's one of the toughest guys you'd ever meet on playing day. He had a switch in his mind. When it was game day, he was ready to play."

Hawkins's habits were legendary around Columbia, quite the opposite of the reserved Dixon. "I was running the bars and he was in study hall," Hawkins told the *Post and Courier* in 2008. "But we got along great." Dixon laughed and said he still does not understand how Hawkins was able to balance his social and football calendars. "He abused his body, having a good time, and still gave 100 percent," Dixon said. "It defies the imagination. He's one of the best friends and teammates I ever had. And from the poker parlor to the football field, he was a competitor."

Together, Dixon and Hawkins helped the Gamecocks rush for 262 yards. Clemson finished with 233 *total* yards. Hawkins got his touchdown. Dixon had one, too. "I remember the end of that ballgame and what a joy it was," Dixon said. "It was a great release for us. None of us had ever got in the end zone against them. It meant a lot to me. I got a game ball from that."

Writers from across the state and country lauded the upset victory for Carolina, which went on to a 7-3 season and finished the year ranked thirteenth in the country. Some columnists admitted that they never saw the result coming. "My mother always told me never to speak with my mouth half-full," wrote Ed Campbell of the *News and Courier* in Charleston. "Right now, I've two skinny jaws full of crow and am speechless."

Howard's sparring partner, Giese, received a heap of praise for his part in the victory.

"Never has a man become more popular in sixty minutes of football than Warren Giese," Red Canup of the *Anderson Independent* said.

It was Giese's first win against the Tigers. And the only one in five tries, as it turned out. But that one victory was enough to humble the sunburned Howard for a day. "They carried the fight to us, and we didn't respond," he told *The State*. "That's all there was to it. They richly deserve their victory."

8

FAREWELL TO A FRIEND

1959

I F THERE'S ANOTHER PERSON who played for NFL coaching legends Vince Lombardi, Tom Landry and George Halas, Gary Barnes is not aware of him.

Barnes earned that distinction in the 1960s while playing for the Green Bay Packers, Dallas Cowboys and Chicago Bears. Those experiences, plus a later stint with a brand-new Atlanta Falcons franchise, gave him a wealth of memorable moments and settings from an NFL career that followed his time as a star receiver at Clemson.

Barnes's biggest thrill as a professional might've been his presence in Yankee Stadium for the 1962 NFL championship game. The Packers, led by Bart Starr, Jim Taylor and Ray Nitschke, won 16–7 that day over a New York Giants team that boasted such luminaries as Y.A. Tittle, Frank Gifford and Sam Huff.

Another unforgettable moment came four years later, when Barnes scored the first touchdown in Falcons history in a game against the Los Angeles Rams.

But none of that—nothing—compares to October 22, 1959, when last rites were administered to a tradition that is treasured to this day. "Of all the games and all the stadiums and all the atmospheres I've been in, to this day I've never seen anything quite like that," Barnes said. "That was something very, very special."

Gary Barnes, an Alabama native who lettered as a receiver at Clemson from 1959 to 1961. He helped the Tigers finish number eleven nationally in 1959. *Courtesy of Clemson University Sports Information Department.*

BIG THURSDAY WAS SO much a part of the culture and fabric of South Carolina that many people, unable to conceive of life without the annual October ritual, were dismissive of the momentum that ultimately brought its end.

The movement was more than a decade in the making, fueled by Clemson's frustration with various inequities that came from the game being staged near Carolina's campus. Ticket allocations were not evenly split. Clemson did not get money from concessions or program sales. And on top of all that, coach Frank Howard and his players had to occupy the sideline that drew direct sunlight.

Howard griped about the arrangement at times in the late 1940s, both publicly in the papers and privately to his team.

"We thought it was ridiculous to play our rival in Columbia every year," said Phil Prince, a senior on Howard's undefeated 1948 team. "And it was even worse that we had to play on a Thursday, which fouled up the schedule. These were all arguments Coach Howard would use later. There was a lot of resentment, because it was patently unfair to have to all of a sudden play a game on a Thursday in the middle of a season against a heavy rival."

Big Thursday grew in importance after the Second World War, to the point that the demand for tickets was said to exceed supply by four times the stadium's capacity. From 1945 to 1954, Clemson enjoyed just one victory over Carolina. The belief among Big Thursday adherents was that Howard's desire for something different would diminish once his Tigers started winning again.

But when Clemson dispatched Carolina by a 28–14 score in 1955, Howard began his postgame chat with the press by amplifying his message. "I still think the game should be played at the last of the season," he said. "Put that down first."

THE CONTRACT FOR BIG Thursday was up the next year, and Howard wanted the new agreement to be a home-and-home arrangement that allowed Clemson and its surrounding community to benefit from the game's popularity. He said Carolina had been "using the Big Thursday game to sell its season tickets and to practically support its entire athletic program, and it's going to stop."

Bob Bradley, longtime sports information director at Clemson and a member of the school's prestigious Ring of Honor, told a newspaper reporter decades later that football interest in the state dropped "like a lead balloon" in the weeks after the teams' October confrontations. "When those two teams played on Big Thursday, the football season was over in this state," he said.

A State of Disunion

In November 1955, a letter from Howard to Clemson's student newspaper ran on the front page of the *Tiger* on homecoming weekend. The coach also called for a new stadium that would be a vast upgrade over Memorial Stadium's 20,654-seat capacity:

> *Every other year this game should be at Clemson so that people from all over the state could see our place and realize the opportunities available here. By playing this game one year at Clemson and one year in Columbia our Atlantic Coast Conference schedule could be worked out more easily and the Clemson home schedule would be fine every year. As things now stand, we have a fine home schedule on odd years but I am not proud of our home schedule on even years.*

The Tigers won again in 1956, beating the Gamecocks 7–0, and Howard continued his charge for change. A few days after the game, sports columnist Jake Penland wrote in *The State* that Howard and IPTAY, the athletics department's fundraising arm, had "taken the lead in a movement to abolish Big Thursday."

"They have advanced some good arguments in favor of the change," Penland wrote. "As many good arguments have been raised against a change."

THE ARGUMENTS REACHED AN official level in March 1957, when Clemson made a formal demand to Carolina that the 1960 game be played in Clemson, with all games thereafter on a home-and-home basis. A tentative date for the first game in Clemson—November 12, 1960—was set. Carolina reacted by releasing news that it had opened negotiations with North Carolina for a long-term contract to fill the void on state fair week.

Time was running out because the 1960 schedules were being arranged quickly, and Clemson had already announced that it scheduled a game at North Carolina State for state fair week. Yet there was still some hope of salvaging Big Thursday, still some people who believed the grand event would never be abolished.

The following appeared in a March 28, 1957 editorial in *The State*:

> *The State still hopes something can be done, but those who have the final say at Clemson are so determined to alternate the game that the chances are they will continue to demand that beginning in 1960 the contest be played there one year and Columbia the next.*

Happily Carolina is not going to leave the public without a big Fair Week game—in fact there is one in mind that in time might become a bigger one than the one with Clemson—The Battle of Carolinas. Carolina and Clemson are the logical opponents on Big Thursday, and in our opinion those who are so headstrong in breaking up their meeting at the State Fair, no matter how well intentioned they are, are doing both institutions and the public a disservice.

Carolina said it wouldn't venture to Clemson until the Tigers offered more seats, and Clemson's trustees approved an increase in capacity to 40,000. Carolina Stadium offered 33,908 seats, but a $300,000 enlargement was planned to add 7,000 more.

CLEMSON WAS ALSO CONFRONTING a complicated, difficult issue that had nothing to do with its rivals in Columbia. The Hartwell Dam project, authorized by Congress in 1950, would bring power generation, flood control and recreation with a reservoir covering 55,950 acres and more than 950 miles of shoreline. The twisting, muddy Seneca River that snaked along the western outskirts of Clemson would eventually be replaced by a scenic lake.

But in the late 1950s, the ramifications of the proposed project put large swaths of Clemson's campus in the crosshairs of catastrophic flooding. Included was Memorial Stadium, which would have been under eighteen feet of water. Thus, there were discussions about building a new stadium off campus, near Anderson Highway. Critics of that idea didn't like the thought of thousands of out-of-town visitors attending games without seeing the beauty of Clemson's campus.

Led by president Robert C. Edwards, Clemson successfully protected itself. The original plan was altered to include two dikes in Clemson that diverted the water west of the areas that had previously been threatened. Filling of the lake later began in 1961.

A bill introduced in March 1957 by Senator John D. Long of Union called for the game to be permanently played in the state fair setting that had made it an institution. The bill also would have required Clemson and Carolina to schedule The Citadel annually beginning in 1958. "Since the taxpayers are paying for the music," Long said at the time, "I think their representatives should be allowed to call some of the tunes."

But the Big Thursday song was headed irrevocably toward its final stanza. The 1958 game, in which the Gamecocks pulled off a stunning

26–6 demolition of the tenth-ranked Tigers, unfolded with most observers aware that the next year's rendition would be the last. In an interview with the *Columbia Record* before the 1959 season, Howard said the state fair arrangement was patently unfair to the Tigers. Clemson would take a 32-21-3 overall record over the Gamecocks into the 1959 game.

"We have been taking our teams down there since before the turn of the century," Howard told the *Record*. "I don't care what people say, the home club definitely has an advantage. Every year we get less than half the tickets. We have the sun field each year and we do not share in the program sales or the concession profits. Besides not having the home field advantage every other year, I frankly don't see a thing fair about the game as far as Clemson is concerned."

GARY BARNES, THE FORMER Clemson receiving star who went on to play for the Packers, Cowboys and Bears, vividly remembers the anticipation and electricity that surrounded the final Big Thursday. Barnes, now a municipal court judge in Clemson, grew up in Alabama just twenty minutes from Auburn's campus. He thought the Alabama-Auburn rivalry was big until he experienced Big Thursday for the first and only time as a sophomore in 1959.

"The crowd for that game was unbelievable," Barnes recalled.

> *When we went on the field to warm up, we had to turn sideways just to get through the entrance to the field because there were so many people jammed in there. There were folding chairs all over the sidelines. It was just really something, not just the size of the crowd but the attitude of the crowd. It was a very special game. It was so loud. There was just something in the air, something I had not seen before and have not seen since.*
>
> *I don't think that game has ever risen to the spectacular event that it was. As big as it is now, it's lost something along the way. And I think you have to be one of the old guys to completely appreciate what I'm saying.*

Coleman Glaze was a freshman in 1959 and had played in the rain-soaked freshman game the night before at Carolina Stadium. He stood on the sidelines for the final Big Thursday and remembered the atmosphere as "electric."

Five days earlier in Clemson, the varsity was scrimmaging against the freshman team at Riggs Field. The varsity, which was ranked seventeenth nationally after a 3-1 start that included an opening triumph over number twelve North Carolina, was sluggish. The freshmen scored the first time they had the ball, and Howard wasn't happy.

"Those guys didn't want to be out there," Glaze recalls. "They were going through the motions. Coach Howard stops practice and says, 'OK freshmen, you're done for the day.' Then he scrimmaged the first and second units for three hours. I mean, he worked them to death."

IN SUNDAY'S EDITIONS OF the *Greenville News*, four days before the big game, Howard told sports columnist Jim Anderson that he was "very happy" to see the end of Big Thursday because the setting gave the Gamecocks "about a two-touchdown advantage."

Howard was proposing a doubleheader game for Saturday of state fair week, combining Carolina's anticipated game against North Carolina with a Clemson game versus Georgia.

An aerial picture from the 1960 game in Clemson a year later—Carolina's first trip to Memorial Stadium. The Tigers won 12–2. *Courtesy of Special Collections, Clemson University Libraries.*

"I think if I brought my Clemson Tigers down there we would provide a big crowd for them, and have three states represented. We would have everybody in South Carolina, and others from Georgia and North Carolina going to see the doubleheader."

Years later, when he was no longer coaching or running Clemson's athletics department, Howard said the doubleheader deal was a done deal before Carolina nixed it. He claimed the Gamecocks were afraid of being outdrawn by Clemson in their own stadium.

Howard caused a stir a few days before the 1959 game when, in the midst of squabbles over ticket distribution for the 1960 and 1961 games, he professed his opinion that the rivalry end altogether. Edwards, the Clemson president and a strong advocate for athletics during a tenure that stretched from 1958 to 1979, quelled fears by expressing confidence that an agreement for future games would be worked out.

The Gamecocks also carried a 3-1 record into Big Thursday, and the state's sportswriters viewed the game as a tossup. Fourth-year Carolina coach Warren Giese, however, was concerned about injuries that chipped away at the Gamecocks' depth and created "a very big problem." He said Clemson, which was trying to duplicate its 1958 ACC title, had the "strongest personnel of any team in the Atlantic Coast Conference." He predicted the Tigers would have "something new offensively."

CAROLINA BASED ITS OFFENSIVE approach on a plodding running game. Clemson was more versatile, thanks in part to the addition of Barnes, who gave the Tigers' offense the receiving threat it had lacked the previous season in falling just short of a national title. Clemson quarterbacks Harvey White and Lowndes Shingler were regarded as two of the best in the ACC.

After the heavy rains Wednesday night, more precipitation was forecast for Big Thursday. It would have been fitting, given that the first meeting between the two schools in 1896 was played beneath a steady rain.

The State marked the passing of an era with solemn words. A photo caption on page 1A spoke of "a time of joy and a time for tears." An editorial chronicled "almost universal" feelings among fans of both schools that the state would lose "a great deal" with the end of Big Thursday.

"The Big Thursday game brought reams of publicity throughout the nation—it was the one day a year that South Carolina shared the football spotlight with no other collegiate teams. Equally a part of the tradition were the social and political activities that had become substantial appendages.

Big Thursday's game had become a sort of South Carolina homecoming—something of a statewide 'family reunion.'"

The State also said Big Thursday "has probably left more vivid and varied memories on more people than any single event in the life of South Carolina."

In Charleston, the *News and Courier* noted that the state legislature would have the "sad duty of repealing what may be the most popular statute in the state—one that makes Thursday of fair week an official holiday."

Even the *Greenville News*, which supported Clemson's desire for a home-and-home agreement, lamented the occasion:

> *Perhaps it had grown into rather too great importance. Certainly it was not just another football game. If there is such a thing in today's high pressure, win-at-all costs atmosphere of intercollegiate rivalry. And a ticket to the game has become a prime goal of the status seekers in a mad scramble comparable only to the fight within the Pentagon for tickets to the Army-Navy game.*
>
> *Still, for all its inflated importance, we mourn the passing of Big Thursday. We are proud of our state and were perhaps foolishly vain about the national attention it brought us on this one day of the year. And we admit to a rigid preference for anything with a long and honorable history. It may not have always been good football, but it never lacked excitement. There's too little like it in the world today and we, along with thousands of other South Carolinians, shall miss it.*

THE MORNING OF BIG Thursday was marked by word-of-mouth news of tragedy in the Upstate. Three Clemson College students from Spartanburg were on their way to the game when their 1953 Pontiac struck the railing of a bridge and swerved into the path of a tractor trailer. The three students, all twenty years old, were thrown from the car and killed instantly.

The weather was unseasonably cool and overcast. The heavy rains that caused havoc with the state fair on Wednesday gave way to a steady drizzle Wednesday morning. It stopped at about noon, two hours before kickoff.

Clemson was allotted 17,960 tickets for the 1959 game and South Carolina, 24,557. Clemson was allowed to bring 1,660 chair seats that were placed on the Tigers' side of the field.

About an hour before kickoff, a fight broke out at midfield between freshmen students from both schools after a Carolina student snagged an orange "rat" cap from the head of a Clemson freshman and scooted off. The Carolina contingent was not pleased to see a Clemson student carrying a live rooster around the stadium.

A special souvenir program that cost a dollar was on sale that day, but there weren't many buyers among Clemson fans. Howard urged Tigers supporters to boycott the program in protest of inequities in the proceeds. He also asked them to hold off on buying soft drinks and other concessions.

Giese had spent two weeks conducting practices in secrecy, barring reporters and others from the outside. He set up television cameras at the stadium that would provide a feed to a closed-circuit TV under a tent near the Carolina bench. He also ordered a special camera installed under the scoreboard that would provide still shots for him to ascertain important information from different angles as the game progressed.

All the technology in the world couldn't save the Gamecocks on this day. Clemson closed Big Thursday with a staggering 27–0 annihilation that was the most lopsided margin of victory Howard had enjoyed in twenty trips to Columbia.

An estimated crowd of forty-seven thousand attended the game, but Gamecock fans began to file out in droves with eight minutes remaining. Giese had stopped consulting his high-tech TV rig a few minutes earlier, with the score 19–0. Led by White, Clemson completed eleven passes for 186 yards while repeatedly burning the Gamecocks for big plays on third down.

WITH A FEW MINUTES remaining, a photographer approached Howard on the sideline and asked to take his picture. Howard suggested waiting until after the game and snapping the photo in the stands to document all the empty seats Gamecocks fans left behind. The image of Howard blowing a goodbye kiss to Big Thursday became one of the most iconic and defining in the rivalry's history.

A group of Clemson fans descended to the field after it was over and tore down the goal posts, both of which were rooted in concrete. They reportedly carried the remains to a nearby steakhouse, found a hacksaw and sold them in individual pieces for five dollars apiece.

Ed Campbell, sports columnist for the *News and Courier*, pecked out this description of the postgame scene:

> *There was a depressing finality about it all. Thousands of discarded newspapers fluttered in and out among the 45,000 now-empty seats...At*

Frank Howard gives a joyous goodbye kiss to Big Thursday after leading his Tigers to a 27–0 smashing of the Gamecocks on October 22, 1959. *Courtesy of Special Collections, Clemson University Libraries.*

either end of the playing field lay twisted remains of what 20 minutes before had been goal posts. Clusters of people, some deliriously happy and others sad to the point of tears, stood on the gridiron. And on the scoreboard in the gathering darkness, written in glittering neon lights, was the epitaph for 1959's Big Thursday—the last one: "Clemson 27, South Carolina 0."

Furman Bisher of the *Atlanta Journal* attended the game and filed a column with the headline "Last Rites for a Friend":

From Wampee to Walhalla, from Yemassee to Tamassee, this little drama of the dawn was enacted. Fathers, mothers, daughters and sons; alumni, alumnae and spirited affiliates; politicians, storekeepers and bankers; lawyers, bakers and thieves; also alcoholics, teetotalers, preachers and bartenders were all going the same way.

There was a funeral of an old friend to attend. The funeral of Big Thursday.

9

YANKING THE TIGERS' TAILS

1961

CARROLL GRAY WRESTLED WITH his nerves as he approached South Carolina coach Marvin Bass on the team's flight to Virginia, where the Gamecocks would play the following day. The student newspaper's sports editor took a breath and tapped Bass on the shoulder. He had a pitch to make.

Earlier in the week, Gray and his Sigma Nu brothers had cooked up a plan for a doozy of a joke. It was innocent, in their minds. The punch line was at Clemson's expense, which made it even better to them. Fraternities were always trying to one-up one another with these gags, and this one would be tough to top.

They would borrow uniforms from Orangeburg High, which featured the same hue as Clemson, and masquerade the next week as the Tigers for a few minutes during pregame warm-ups. The Sigma Nus would have their fun, create some comedy and then clear the field before the real Tigers emerged. Gray sold Bass on it being "good, clean fun."

"Well, that sounds innocent enough," Bass told Gray, sort of chuckling at the idea of the gag. What the first-year coach did not realize was that he had just signed off on quite possibly the biggest prank in college football history—and something that would incite a fairly large mob scene on the Carolina Stadium turf.

Gray returned from the trip to Virginia, where the Gamecocks lost 28–20, and let his brothers know the prank was given a thumbs-up by Bass, who provided resources such as a place for the students to dress and pads to shove inside the uniforms. The school's honor society was aware and supportive, as well.

Like the actual players in the 1961 game, the Sigma Nus wanted to be prepared. They had a couple of dress rehearsals on the intramural fields and all sorts of meetings throughout the week leading up to the game. "We really just hoped for the best," said Ed Hancock, one of the brothers, a freshman in 1961. "We thought, 'If we're sharp enough, look good enough, we can pull this thing off.'"

Part of the trick of it all was staying quiet during those days before the game. When you're sitting on that kind of a secret, it can be difficult to keep it a secret—and especially when so many social creatures are in on it. "We were afraid, or even pretty sure, someone would get drunk, tell their girlfriend, who would tell someone at Clemson," Hancock said. "We just knew it would get out."

It didn't, though. Somehow, the fraternity kept its lips zipped. "I believe that's the last secret that was ever kept at the University of South Carolina," said another Sigma Nu, Herbert Adams, who is now a university trustee. "No one knew what was happening."

As the game got closer, Adams said his anxiety level increased. The fraternity could not be sure how this was going to go. "I remember being concerned," he said. "I wondered if it'd be funny or just turn into bedlam."

Ready or not, Saturday arrived. It was show time.

CLEMSON HAS THE HILL. South Carolina has "2001." Entrances have become a part of the football fabric and tradition at the two schools. But they have never had a pregame entrance like the South Carolina Sigma Nus, dressed as the Clemson Tigers, in 1961.

The Clemson fans jumped to their feet and roared as the fraternity brothers ran onto the field to the sounds of "Tiger Rag." "Their band was playing like hell," Hancock said. "They didn't expect anything like that. Why would you?"

On the Clemson sideline, Whitey Jordan sat on a bench and watched the chicanery unfold. He coached the freshman team and was able to leave the locker room early as the varsity made its final preparations.

Jordan was one of the few people in the stadium who knew instantly that this was a ruse.

"The crowd roared when they came out," Jordan recalled, "but the uniforms weren't right. They were a different color. I recognized it immediately."

Fans of both schools somehow missed the fact that the Sigma Nus, in some cases, did not exactly cut athletic figures. "Some of them looked like football players, but we had some guys out there in uniforms that were five-five, five-six," said Gray, who was watching everything transpire from the stands. "We had some guys with kneepads dragging the ground."

As the players trotted out, so did Sigma Nu Ronald Leitch. He was wearing a fedora and a suit, with a pillow shoved underneath his shirt to represent a belly. Leitch was Frank Howard. He looked the part of the cantankerous Clemson coach—and acted it, too. A woman in the crowd yelled, "Coach Howard, I love you!" Leitch, smacking on bubble gum to mimic Howard's chaw of tobacco, shouted back obscenities.

Not everything went precisely to plan. At one point, the Sigma Nus had plotted to trot out a cow with "Miss Clemson" written on its side in white shoe polish. It was supposed to enter alongside Leitch's Frank Howard character. The press box announcer was to ask if there was a butcher in the house.

The cow did not cooperate. It died on a wagon in the parking lot. Naturally, that part was cut from the program.

Dead cow aside, Hancock remembered thinking that everyone in the seats was really buying the act. That was both good and bad. The moment of clarity was on its way. It would provide pure joy for the Gamecocks—and inspire rage inside the Tigers. The show, though, had to go on. They had gone this far with it, after all. The Sigma Nus launched into the act they had diligently practiced.

The imposters paired off for warm-up drills, which is when it started to become obvious that this was a stunt. The Sigma Nus started helping each other stretch, even milking one another's thumbs like a farmer would a cow.

The public address system, also in on the prank, popped on a Chubby Checker record, and the "Tigers" started doing "The Twist." Meanwhile, Hancock, equipped with a strange talent, began punting the ball backward. Standing in the end zone, he would kick the ball ten or twenty yards over his head into the crowd, much to the fans' confusion. Soon after, Hancock's brothers joined him in the end zone, and everyone did a dance called the Hully Gully, what Adams later called "the most prissified dance you've ever seen."

And that did it. The Clemson fans were slowly coming around. The Hully Gully sealed the fact that they'd been had. They didn't like it, either. Hancock said it looked like a "huge, orange sheet of plastic melting and pouring out on the field" as masses of Clemson freshmen, wearing the signature orange "Rat" caps, scrambled to the field to exact justice.

"They always had security for those games, but it wasn't very good," said Jordan, the Clemson freshman coach. "They had a fence about three feet high around the field, and kids could just put a hand on it and jump it."

Adams made note of the fact that Clemson, as a school, had a majority of males in 1961. It was not that far removed from its military history, either. "If there were four hundred fans, there were four hundred guys," said Adams, who added that he was glad he was in the bleachers. "And they were mean."

The Sigma Nus did have a contingency for that kind of thing. They were to run to a safe house of sorts, an equipment closet under the stadium. After taking a few punches and shoves, the brothers eventually made it, leaving the Carolina and Clemson fans out on the field, still fighting. The teams' cheerleaders, afraid, took cover under a wooden platform between the field and bleachers. It was a weird, wild scene, everyone brawling. The game was delayed for about a half hour while police officers restored order, but the fighting would resume at the game's conclusion. Jordan remembers the team's doctors spending hours in the locker room after the game sewing up students who'd been injured in the postgame melee.

"The students didn't leave," Jordan said. "They just fought and fought and fought. A lot of people got beat up that day, and they just kept bringing them in with cuts and all."

THE SIGMA NU BROTHERS certainly made their imprint for posterity, but the game wasn't so bad, either.

"It Was the Wildest," *The State* headline proclaimed in its Sunday editions. And that had nothing to do with the prank, which was not even mentioned in the newspaper until Monday. The game was plenty wacky enough.

Clemson entered as the favorite, although the Tigers had just three victories at that point. Their four losses, though, had come by an average of 5.2 points a game, and they had not been defeated by any more than 10 points. South Carolina had only two victories in seven outings, a 10–7 win at Wake Forest and a 20–10 victory against Maryland.

The teams might not have been national, or even conference, contenders, but they did put on an entertaining show for the first game at Carolina Stadium after the end of Big Thursday. South Carolina trailed 14–13 in the fourth quarter, but it eventually scored the game-winning touchdown by making the best of a bad play.

Fullback Dick Day was stood up at the line of scrimmage. He fumbled. The football went squirting out to the left, and Clemson could not locate it.

Jim Costen, South Carolina's quarterback, found the ball. He picked it up and ran in for a twenty-five-yard touchdown. Billy Gambrell scored a two-point conversion to give the Gamecocks a 21–14 cushion.

The Tigers were twice stopped inside Carolina territory in the final minutes. The Gamecocks halted Clemson at the one-yard line on one occasion. A Gambrell interception in the last few seconds then ended the game. "I've lost a lot of games in my life and I've won a lot," Howard told *The State*, "but I don't think I ever lost one like this."

Probably not, no. After all, how many times had he ever been impersonated on the field by the other team's students?

The following Monday morning, a police officer appeared at the Sigma Nu residence hall, asking for Gray. The officer had a letter from school administrators, summoning Gray for a meeting at 2:00 p.m. that day. Far more anxious than when he had walked up to Bass on the airplane, Gray assumed he would be expelled for his role in the events. Bass had told William Patterson, then the school's chief administrative officer and later a university president, that it was all the Sigma Nus' doing. He did not mention giving the brothers his blessing.

That left Gray to face the music. He nervously did his best to explain, bracing for the worst. Patterson listened. Not known for showing much emotion, an ever-so-slight smile started to inch across his face.

"Don't do it again," Patterson said. "Get out of here."

Gray and his brothers had officially pulled off the prank.

10

THE WIN THAT WASN'T

1965

A COUPLE HUNDRED DOLLARS. IN 1965, that was the difference between the first conference championship in South Carolina's history and the embarrassment the school endured the following year as a result of having that title publicly stripped.

A thrilling 17–16 victory against Clemson brought great joy to Columbia, where the Gamecocks shared the ACC championship with Duke. The following summer, just before the 1966 season began, it was taken away as a result of three players receiving extra benefits.

The players were never named, though they were not believed to be integral parts of the team. *The State*, citing a school source, said the infraction involved each one receiving between $75 and $100 for meals and books. The Gamecocks celebrated a conference championship like kings, only to have that dream season stricken from the record books because of a relatively small amount of money going toward things required for education.

Clemson and North Carolina State wound up sharing the ACC title, with 5-2 records. By no fault of its own, Duke, at 4-2, also lost its share of the title. The Tigers and Wolfpack picked up a win because they lost to the Gamecocks, but the Devils had already defeated Carolina.

After the switch, parades were not exactly thrown in Raleigh and the Upstate. North Carolina State's players did not receive their rings until 2011, forty-six years later. It was charity in which Tigers coach Frank Howard was not interested. "That's bad," he told *The State*. "All I know is the score of our game will always read 17–16, South Carolina's favor."

Howard never said another word about the awarded championship of 1965. There was a reason why that was the case.

A State of Disunion

EVEN THOUGH IT ULTIMATELY backed into the title, Clemson had three different chances to claim it late in the season. The Tigers were 5-2 overall and 4-0 in the league when they lost 17–13 on the road at North Carolina. They returned home and lost 6–0 to Maryland.

By then, dropping to 5-4 and 4-2 in the ACC, the door had been opened for several teams, including the Gamecocks. There were five different scenarios in which any number of teams could win a piece of the title, although Clemson still remained the only one that could win it outright entering the rivalry game at Carolina Stadium.

As a result of Clemson's late-season slide, the game with Carolina took on new importance. It was the only time the teams would decide a conference championship on the field, before Carolina eventually broke apart in 1971 to become an independent. The rivalry was typically fascinating for tradition's sake alone. Now it meant something more. Virginia coach George Blackburn told *The State* that he would "pay double the price to watch these two teams go after each other." North Carolina State coach Earle Edwards called it a coin flip, a fifty-fifty proposition.

The previous year had to be factored in as fuel, too. Clemson held a 3–0 lead virtually the entire game, until the Gamecocks magically reeled off a ninety-three-yard drive in the final minutes to escape with a 7–3 victory. Tigers fullback Pat Crain was stopped inches from the winning score in the final seconds. They were still smarting a year later.

"We are tired of hearing Gamecock partisans gloat about last year's victory," *Tiger* editor Charles Hill wrote in a column submitted that week to *The State*. "We are tired of seeing pictures in the paper of fullback Pat Crain being stopped at the goal line in Clemson's futile attempt to score. We are tired of looking at last year's score—USC 7, Clemson 3—and knowing it should have been different. So we are determined to win the game this year—we know it must be won."

CAROLINA COMPLETED CLEMSON'S MISERY—UNTIL the ACC's decision the following year, anyway—by defeating the Tigers by the narrowest of margins. Memories of Crain flooded through Clemson's minds as, down 17–10, it faced fourth and goal at the one-foot line in the final moments. Howard boldly called a pass play, and quarterback Thomas Ray found Phil Rogers to bring the Tigers to within one point.

Clemson lined up for the extra-point kick, but holder Jimmy Addison, a backup quarterback, took the snap and rose up to pass. Addison threw

It was common for students at Clemson and Carolina to trek to the opposing campus and vandalize popular monuments. In this photo, likely from the 1960s, Gamecock fans leave their mark on Thomas Green Clemson's statue. *Courtesy of the University of South Carolina Archives, South Caroliniana Library.*

toward Bo Ruffner in the end zone. If Ruffner hauled it in, the 18–17 win would have given Clemson the conference title.

Instead, Carolina's Bob Gunnells got in between the ball and Ruffner, knocking it away to seal the Gamecocks' 17–16 victory and *their* conference championship—a first. Realizing a tie would not help Clemson, Howard had to go for two points. But a fake kick? Some wondered why Howard did not call a conventional play, with his best players on the field. "We came to win and we tried to win," Howard said. "We just didn't make it."

A microcosm of that forgettable November, the Tigers faltered throughout the final game. They were cruising in the second quarter, leading 10–0, when Carolina quarterback Mike Fair found J.R. Wilburn on third and twelve for a fifty-yard gain deep into Clemson territory. Fair had just ninety-four passing yards in the game, but that play, which led to a score, changed the complexion of the game.

A nine-play, fifty-five-yard drive in the fourth quarter ended with Bobby Harris's seven-yard run serving as the winning score. Again, the Tigers had plenty of opportunities to overcome that. In addition to the final sequence, Clemson at one point midway through the fourth quarter rumbled to the Carolina sixteen. Once there, Rogers fumbled, and Stan Juk recovered for the Gamecocks. Later, with Clemson again on the move, Ray was intercepted at the Carolina seven-yard line by Bobby Bryant. Then the Tigers went sixty-three yards on that final touchdown drive, only to fail on the two-point conversion.

The box score read, too, like a Tigers victory. Clemson had nineteen first downs to Carolina's ten. It had 314 total yards, compared to the Gamecocks' 154. And, yet, in that moment, it was Carolina wearing the crown.

"South Carolina can be good in every sport. That's what it deserves," said Gamecocks coach Marvin Bass, then 3-2 against the Tigers in his tenure. "This was a big milestone today. A big one. We're heading in the right direction. Someday this place is going to blossom out and get what it deserves, and when it does it's really going to be something to see."

BASS WAS THERE FOR the rise but not the fall. After five seasons, and insisting after the Clemson victory that he was not going anywhere, he took a job coaching in the Canadian Football League.

Bass departed in April, but he was met at the border by NCAA officials. They were already looking into some possible eligibility issues. Interestingly, Bass's replacement, Paul Dietzel, had tipped off the governing body soon after he took the Carolina job. That did not please Bass. "If I was going to conduct an investigation," he later told *The State*, "I would have had the courtesy to contact the guy who was there before me." Bass later tried to take back that statement, but it was too late. The damage was done, really, on more than one front.

On July 29, 1966, with Dietzel's first season approaching and the 1965 title a memory, Carolina's only conference championship in seventy-one years of playing football was stripped. "We are greatly disturbed at the irregularities which have come to light," school president Thomas Jones said in a statement.

North Carolina State's Edwards had compassion for the Gamecocks, who, for the most part, did not even know any infraction had been committed. "We take no delight in having this happen," said Edwards, coach of one of the new champions. "I felt South Carolina beat us fair and square last season, and I'd much rather win a title on the field where it's supposed to be won. This will help our record, but frankly, I'm real sorry to hear about this."

He added that the Wolfpack also lost to Clemson, so the Tigers were deserving of a larger share of the title. It was a championship no one really wanted after it was lost by the Gamecocks and Devils.

"The history of South Carolina, football especially, is just 'shoulda, coulda, woulda,' 'if only,' or 'what if' or 'man, we were so close.' It's not a real glorious past," Bryant, a Carolina defensive back, told *The State* in 2009. "That's just another chapter on how we screwed something up that should have been, could have been a good chapter."

Bryant, like many others from that team, still has his ACC title ring.

"I wasn't sure if I was supposed to put it on a charm bracelet or put it on a gold chain and wear it around my neck or give it to my girlfriend," Bryant told the newspaper. "I wasn't one for a lot of jewelry and stuff. I look at it once in a while when I go in there to get something out, and I say, 'My little co-championship football that no longer represents what happened.'"

11

UNBLEMISHED

1968–70

S OMETIMES DREAMS DO NOT come true. That is a fact for which Tommy Suggs is thankful.

In the days leading up to the 1969 game against Clemson, South Carolina's senior quarterback dreamed that his first and last home game against the Tigers would end with a loss. Fretting the result, he said he literally lost sleep the Thursday and Friday nights before the game. "I was worried this morning, too," Suggs told reporters after the game. "I couldn't sleep very well and my legs ached."

It was just a dream. In reality, the Gamecocks were two touchdowns better than Clemson in 1969, and Suggs was a big reason why. In truth, it was not even all that trying. Carolina scored the first seventeen points of the game. It sweated a bit when Clemson cut the lead to 17–13 before the half, but the Tigers were held scoreless the rest of the game ("Clemson just could not do anything," Suggs said. "We stuffed them.") and the Gamecocks padded the lead with ten more points.

Suggs had 211 passing yards and fifteen completions, and 122 yards and nine of those passes went to senior Fred Zeigler. Fullback Warren Muir had 127 yards rushing. The Gamecocks were balanced. They gouged the Tigers for 287 rushing yards and 230 passing yards—a total of 517 yards. "We just beat the brains out of them," Suggs said. "We played loose. We really had a big day. It was one of the best days I can remember."

Entering 2011, the Tigers had won four or more games eight different times in the series, including three times since 1988. The longest Clemson streak was seven straight wins from 1934 to 1940. The Tigers, interestingly, won four consecutive games against the Gamecocks in 1897–1900 and 1997–2000.

Meanwhile, South Carolina's longest winning streak was four, from 1951 to 1954. It had only won three straight three other times. That is all noteworthy in this context for one reason: it means something when the Gamecocks get on any sort of modest streak in the series against Clemson. The players in those games become folk heroes, some of the all-time greats in the program's history. If you defeat Clemson, you are in a fraternity of sorts at Carolina. If you beat them two or three times? You're effectively deities. The 1969 Carolina team qualifies on multiple levels, then, since it also still stands as the only conference champion in the school's history.

It MADE SENSE WHY Suggs feared a letdown against the Tigers. The previous week, the Gamecocks had gone to Wake Forest and, in front of twenty-five thousand people, won a 24–6 game that clinched the ACC title for Carolina. It believed it had won the league four years earlier, only to have that championship eventually stripped. This one stuck.

"It was a big deal for the school and for the team, ourselves," said Zeigler, who walked on and left as, at the time, the school's all-time leader in catches (146) and yards (1,876). "We could legitimately say that, finally, we'd won it. We were all aware of what a breakthrough that was."

The sense, he added, was that it was just the beginning of something. With the initial title, surely there would be others. That's what the players and coach Paul Dietzel presumed, Dietzel having arrived in Columbia just in time to hand back the ACC crown Carolina had claimed in 1965. The circumstances made the euphoria in 1969 all the more grand. "I've never experienced a more thrilling day in my life," Dietzel told reporters, "because I see it for what it is—a beginning."

Years later, Zeigler could only laugh at that perception, one he believed wholeheartedly then. "Not so much, I guess," Zeigler said with the knowledge that, entering 2011, there was still only one conference title banner hanging inside Williams-Brice Stadium. (The Gamecocks did at least play for a conference title, the SEC championship, in 2010.)

With the ACC title secured, Dietzel, then 1-2 against the Tigers at Carolina, urged his team to remain focused on Clemson. That became doubly difficult because bowl possibilities were swirling around the team

Tommy Suggs remains the only quarterback in Carolina history to ever go 3-0 in his varsity career against Clemson. *Courtesy of Tommy Suggs.*

early that week. Reporters, fed with info from the team, thought a win against the Tigers was required for a bowl invite.

The Peach Bowl did not wait, however, extending an offer to the Gamecocks on that Monday. Carolina accepted, putting even less meaning on the Clemson game. As a result, the Gamecocks had a most weak week of practice.

"Back then, you know, hell, there were no bowl games," Suggs said. "That was big. We were going nuts. I was actually scared we would be overconfident. And I really had stomach problems, just worried about it."

A strange quality about that 1969 team emerged that week, though: it could be good in games, big games, even with a poor week of preparation. Dietzel said to *The State*, "I told the team after the game, 'Now you can talk about the Peach Bowl.'" The victory against Clemson capped a perfect 6-0 conference season for the Gamecocks, making them only the fifth team at that time to go undefeated in ACC play.

Frank Howard, the Tigers' coach and icon, said this after coaching his last game against the Gamecocks and closing his career with back-to-back losing seasons: "Really, they got a purty good team."

FOR SUGGS, THE VICTORY was the second against Clemson—and third, if you count the 1967 freshman team's win at Death Valley. When Howard recruited Suggs, from just outside Lamar, South Carolina, he reminded Suggs he could play—and beat—Carolina three times at Death Valley. Howard did not foresee that ploy one day working against him.

What intrigued Suggs in the recruiting process was what could happen after his college career, not during it. On a visit to Columbia, Carolina trotted out several wealthy businessmen for Suggs to meet. They told him he could choose any profession at their school and find success. (That turned out to be accurate for Suggs, too. He went on to co-own a prominent insurance business in downtown Columbia.)

Suggs told Howard, and specifically assistant Art Baker, no thanks. He did the same to Lefty Driesell, who was recruiting him to play basketball at Davidson. Oddly enough, Clemson seemed to understand, but Driesell did not. Suggs, though, was meant to play football at Carolina.

The freshman game between the Gamecocks and Tigers set the tone for the following three years. With the Gamecocks up a couple of scores, Clemson faced a fourth and one and called a timeout.

The Carolina defense was so fired up that it ran over toward the Clemson sideline and actually encouraged the Tigers to go for the first down. They did go for it. And the defense caused Clemson fullback Jim Sursavage to fumble.

The following year, as a member of the varsity team, Suggs led an offense that romped up and down the field against Clemson. One problem: for whatever reason, the Gamecocks could not manage to score. The Carolina defense allowed just one Tigers field goal, extending the game long enough for defensive back Tyler Hellams to return a punt seventy-three yards in the final minutes for the game's lone touchdown in a 7–3 Gamecocks victory. A win was a win. Defensive back Pat Watson later told *The State* that the team was "brave enough to throw Dietzel in the shower afterward." South Carolina finished 4-6 in 1968, but that Clemson victory, sloppy as it was, capped a 4-3 season in the ACC and provided hope for the following season.

Leaving Death Valley after that upset victory, the coaches told the players to put on their helmets as they headed to the locker room. They did not immediately understand why, but they did soon enough.

"Two fairly nice-looking women swung very heavy aluminum seats at me," Suggs said, "and hit me in the head. I don't mean to condemn all Clemson fans for that, but that happened to me. It was different back then. It was just crazy."

The win was bittersweet for Suggs, who had been emotional all week knowing his only brother was leaving that Sunday for Vietnam and the long, frustrating, deadly conflict there. He was scheduled to leave Wednesday, but the family negotiated for him to be able to stay through the weekend, so he could see his brother start and play against Clemson.

Suggs considered that victory, his first of three as a varsity player, a going-away present, even if it came by the narrowest of margins.

THE CLEMSON FANS DID not like Suggs and the Gamecocks any more by the time they returned to Death Valley in 1970. If anything, though, they were lulled into a false sense of security by that Carolina team.

Coming off the 1969 conference title, it began the year ranked seventeenth in the country, one of only six times in the program's history that the Gamecocks have started a season in the polls. That looked wise when Carolina started the year 3-1-1, with a three-point loss at Georgia Tech the only real blemish.

However, that is when a rash of injuries hit and spread through the team, decimating it in Suggs's senior season. Suggs hurt his ankle in the 7–7 tie at North Carolina State, the third game of the season, but he gutted through the rest of the schedule. The Gamecocks started sinking with an October 17 loss to Maryland, and by the time Duke defeated them 42–38 on November 14, they were on a five-game losing streak. A bowl bid was beyond out of the question. The only game left in Suggs's career was Clemson. The Gamecocks were in salvage mode.

Going into that 1970 game, Suggs admits he did at least consider the fact that he was putting his perfect 3-0 mark against Clemson on the line. "I do remember getting nervous the week of my senior year and thinking, 'Gosh, you know, I've never lost to them. Ever. This game's important,'" Suggs said. "I hadn't really thought about it up to that point. As the week went on, I got more nervous about it." But this was coming from the guy who lost sleep the year before and everything worked out all right. Why not one more time?

The first half resembled a delayed reaction of his dream from the previous year. Suggs threw three interceptions, putting an already banged-up defense in bad positions. South Carolina trailed. When Dietzel was unhappy with Suggs, he would call him "Tom." He got that treatment at halftime.

"He's standing there," Suggs said, "and I walked in and he said, 'Well, Tom, you're eight for eight—five to us, three to them.' I thought, 'Well, shoot.'"

Turned out, Suggs was incorrectly reading Clemson's linebackers. He made an adjustment, and suddenly everything became easier in the second half. Instead of three interceptions, Suggs tossed three touchdown passes. "He was one smart player," Zeigler said. "If you didn't have a good defense, he would work you over." A ten-yard throw that ended in a fifty-yard touchdown to Jimmy Mitchell sealed a 38–32 victory to give the Gamecocks a little better feeling to end a difficult 4-6-1 season.

It also signaled a 4-0 career for Suggs against the Tigers, three as a varsity player and one as a freshman. Three of the four wins were on enemy turf, too. "I never realized it would have the significance that it does now," Suggs said. "Honestly, it shouldn't. There should be five others out there like me. But there aren't. It does mean something. It's something, clearly, that I'm proud of now. No disrespect to Clemson or anybody we played against, but, yeah, it's nice."

12

GRANTZ'S CALLED SHOT

1975

S outh Carolina quarterback Jeff Grantz was walking with teammates and fans to the annual Tiger Burn in 1975 when one of the best athletes in school history noticed a stressed expression on the face of one of the Gamecocks' biggest supporters.

"What's wrong?" Grantz asked R.J. Moore. "You look worried."

Moore, longtime owner of the Exxon station on Rosewood Drive, confirmed it.

"Hell yeah, I'm worried!" he said. "We've got Clemson tomorrow. We've got to win to go to a bowl."

Grantz rolled his eyes and laughed.

"Don't worry, R.J.," he told Moore. "We're going to score every time we've got the football."

The exchange was meant to make Moore feel better. If it didn't for some reason, what happened the following day at Williams-Brice Stadium absolutely did. Grantz and his Gamecocks teammates went out and registered the most decided of South Carolina's thirty-nine victories in the series.

To this day, say "56–20" to a diehard Clemson or Carolina fan and they will know precisely what it means. You will likely get a strong reaction of some kind.

Grantz was true to his word—and then some. The Gamecocks scored each time they had the ball, all right. "Turns out we scored touchdowns every time we had the football," Grantz said. "We didn't have to kick a field goal. I didn't have to punt."

It was not as if the result came altogether unexpectedly, if for no other reason than that Clemson was enduring one of the worst seasons in school history. The Tigers entered the rivalry game 2-8, and injuries had rattled the team to its core.

Still, no one on South Carolina's side expected the Tigers to simply hand the Gamecocks the game. Clemson had played well two weeks earlier, to defeat North Carolina, and it hung with a good Maryland team on the road the week before. The Gamecocks saw a Tigers team playing better ball. "I've really been expecting them to explode every week this season," Carolina senior center Mike McCabe told *The State* that week. "I don't know what their problem has been, but I've been waiting for them to get it all together. That's apparently what they've done the past two weeks."

South Carolina, meanwhile, started the season 5-1 to jump into the polls at number twenty. That was somewhat surprising, since Carolina had been an average 4-7 team in 1974. It might have been underestimated because it had gone through a coaching change, with Paul Dietzel's dismissal and Jim Carlen's hiring. Carlen had led Texas Tech to bowl games in four of the past five seasons, and he had a core of strong senior leaders, including Grantz and McCabe.

The Gamecocks' start to the year was stunted by a 24–6 loss at Louisiana State and then a last-second defeat on TV at North Carolina State. The season threatened to come apart when Appalachian State then came to Columbia and upset the Gamecocks 39–34. It was gut-check time for Carolina and especially its seniors.

A rebound win against Wake Forest got South Carolina to 6-4, and it needed a victory against Clemson for a berth in the Tangerine Bowl. "We felt like we should have been 8-2," Grantz said. "Woulda, shoulda. It doesn't matter, whatever. All that mattered was we had to beat Clemson to get to a bowl."

In addition to raw desire, the Gamecocks also incorporated a few wrinkles the week leading up to the game. Commonplace now but virtually unheard of then, Carolina would put its running back in motion and have him line up in the slot, giving the team four receivers. "We felt like they couldn't cover, couldn't adjust to it," Grantz said. "We all felt really good about the game plan. We were very confident."

Hence, Grantz offered those strong words to Moore on the eve of the game.

GRANTZ GREW UP IN Maryland, far removed from the passion and pageantry of the Big Thursday tradition and the Carolina-Clemson rivalry. He first saw the game up close in 1971, on a recruiting visit hosted by the Gamecocks.

Clemson's coaches ran over to the South Carolina sideline and chided him, letting him know he should be in the Tigers' section and not the rival's. "Right there, first hand, I knew about the rivalry. It was really intense," Grantz said. "All the other games I'd seen before were nothing like that one, you know? You could just see and feel it."

Grantz recalled seeing Carolina quarterbacks throw about a half dozen interceptions in a 17-7 loss to the Tigers. Yeah, the Gamecocks could use him.

A tug of war among a handful of schools, Carolina and Clemson included, ensued. Clemson was ruled out because it did not have the major Grantz desired. When North Carolina learned he picked the Gamecocks, the Tar Heels' coaches told him he "ruined their Christmas."

Grantz's signing was a victory for Carolina in more than one way: he would also be a valuable member of the baseball team, twice helping it to the College World Series while on campus.

Several quarterbacks played Grantz's freshman year, but no one stuck. After a 4-7 season, Dietzel felt that it was time to tweak the offensive system. The Gamecocks would reduce the number of drop-back throwing plays— ones that were successful for Tommy Suggs and the ACC title winners in 1969—and go with more of a veer offense. The passing plays would come more on rollouts and fake handoffs. "As soon as they did that," Grantz said, "I thought, 'Hey, this is me.'"

Grantz became so committed to the offense that, in the spring of 1973, he told baseball coach Bobby Richardson that he wanted to focus on football for the time being. He received Richardson's blessing since he was not playing much as a young outfielder. "If you need me, you know where to find me," Grantz told Richardson.

One day, Richardson called him. Carolina's center fielder had pulled a hamstring. Grantz was needed. "It was the coolest day ever of my life," he said. "We had a scrimmage that Saturday afternoon, and then I played that night in center field. I got a hit, actually."

The opponent? Clemson.

The Tigers were already tiring of Grantz by the end of that year. He made his mark on the football rivalry by running circles around Clemson—in sneakers. Grantz had been gimpy for about a month after bruising an ankle in the LSU game, but there was no way he was missing

Gamecocks quarterback Jeff Grantz, who also played center field for the baseball team, led Carolina to its most resounding victory in the series in 1975. *Courtesy of Mike Safran.*

his first real shot at the Tigers. "I taped it up and put on high white Chuck Taylors," Grantz said with a laugh. "It didn't bother me one bit. They were brand-new, blinding white."

Sneakers probably would not have worked as well on Williams-Brice's current natural grass playing surface, but the concrete-hard artificial turf was a good enough fit. And, well, it was South Carolina's superhero wearing them. "Nothing Jeff ever did surprised me," McCabe said. "He could have been out there in tap shoes and done well. He had that confidence that he'd get the job done. All we had to do was do our job, and he would do his. It was really special playing with him."

The 32–20 victory against the Tigers as an example, the new offense—with Grantz running it—was a success. So it was confusing the following season, in 1974, when Carolina reversed course to finish 4-7, including a 39–21 loss at Clemson. Grantz recalled that Bill Wingo, whose son Scott would later star at Carolina in baseball, intercepted one of his passes. "I remember someone came up to try and block me and I was so mad I threw him down on the ground," Grantz said. "While I was doing that, the guy ran right by me to score a touchdown. Rather than make the tackle, I was too busy being upset. They beat us up there pretty good."

That was Dietzel's last game at Carolina. He was done after nine seasons, finishing 42-53-1 at the school. The seniors rallied around Carlen, his successor. Still, the Gamecocks needed that Clemson game in 1975 to receive a rare postseason bid. It was Grantz's last chance, at both the Tigers and a bowl.

THE STATE CALLED GRANTZ'S finale in the rivalry a "something-to-remember-me-by" performance. People still remember. Clemson cannot forget.

Carolina piled up 458 rushing yards and 626 total yards against the Tigers. In addition to Grantz's play, the Gamecocks also featured two 1,000-yard rushers that season—when they had never even had one previously. Clarence Williams rushed for 160 yards against Clemson, finishing with 1,016 yards in the regular season. Kevin Long had broken the 1,000-yard plateau the previous week at Wake Forest; he finished with 1,114 yards in the regular season.

Grantz added 122 rushing yards, including a 19-yard touchdown run. With that success on the ground, he did not have to throw all that much. He made the most of his throws, though. He completed nine of twelve passes. Five of the nine completions went for touchdowns.

Top receiver Philip Logan had thirteen- and forty-one-yard scoring receptions. Long caught a three-yarder. Randy Chastain had a thirty-four-yard touchdown catch. Stevie Stephens had the other, a nineteen-yarder. It's safe to say, Clemson had no answers for the wrinkle Carolina added that week. "My key would be the strong safety," Grantz said. "If he did this, I'd hit this guy. If he did that, I'd hit that guy."

The Gamecocks led 35–6 at the half, scoring just before the break on a play Grantz said he drew in the dirt with Carlen and Logan. Grantz faked the post-route throw, and Logan broke for the corner. Touchdown. Back-breaker. "That's the first time I ever remember showing much emotion," Grantz said.

Carolina just kept scoring and scoring—one too many times if you ask Clemson's players or fans. The last touchdown came on a Grantz throw with fifty-four seconds left. Tigers quarterback Mike O'Cain was not happy about that after the game. Grantz shrugged. "It was fourth and goal at the twenty-yard line," he said. "What do you do? Kick a field goal? All our plays were called at the line of scrimmage, twenty yards and in. I got up to the line of scrimmage and called a simple out route. The guy makes a diving catch in the corner of the end zone. That put us up 56–20. It was my last game. I wasn't going to stand there and take a knee."

The objective in any game is perfection. For one day, Carolina got close. "It's execution and perfection," McCabe said. "That's what your ultimate goal is. That day was something to see. Someone scored a touchdown every time we had the ball. It made it sweeter that it was against Clemson, obviously."

The Williams-Brice scoreboard indicated that Grantz had set records for single-season total yardage (2,071), total touchdowns (28) and passing touchdowns (16). He left as the school's all-time leader, with fifty-three total scores. "When people ask me when I played, I tell them I was a center for Jeff Grantz," McCabe said. "It was an honor to play with him."

The fifty-six points were, at that time, the most scored by either team in the long-standing series. "I just kept looking up at the scoreboard and going, 'Man, this is an awesome way to go out,'" Grantz said. "That was it. That was my last home game, ever. What better way? We scored every time we had the ball."

On the other sideline, it was a most humbling feeling. Clemson, so dominant in the series, was on unfamiliar territory. It was one more painful wound in a 2-9 season. "I feel like I'm just waking up from a nightmare," the Tigers' Frank Wise told *The State*. "That's what the season has been, a nightmare."

There was a residual effect, though. How exactly it played out internally and externally is up for debate, but Clemson's supporters and administration made it clear that it was not to again happen. The Tigers pumped resources and energy into their football program like never before.

Clemson promptly won seven of the next eight games in the series and claimed the national title in 1981. Grantz, great as that victory was, unknowingly sparked the Tigers' glory days.

"Everyone gets pissed when they lose," he said. "I guess they were more than mad. After that, it was Clemson, Clemson, Clemson. I told my wife I wasn't going to go back to Clemson until we beat them up there, and then I wasn't going back anymore. I didn't get to go back until after Mike Hold and 1984."

13

CLOSE...AND CIGARS

1977

WITH NINETY-NINE SECONDS REMAINING and Clemson at its thirty-three-yard line, Joe Bostic stood in the huddle with a feeling he'd never experienced in a game before and never did thereafter.

Some of Bostic's teammates said afterward that there was perfect calm among the Tigers in the raucous din of Williams-Brice Stadium after they watched a 24–0 lead vanish. Bostic tells a different story.

"In all my times at Clemson or anywhere, I have never been in a game where I thought I was going to throw up," he said. "We were down, it was a TV timeout, and I'm thinking: 'How in God's name have we pissed away this game?'"

The story of this game—and perhaps the most memorable snapshot of the entire rivalry—was Jerry Butler's leaping, twisting touchdown catch of a Steve Fuller heave fifty seconds later that gave the Tigers an epic and stunning 31–27 triumph. But there was more to the game and its implications than one play; a second half filled with unbearably tense moments and wild shifts in momentum left a permanent impression on everyone who played, coached and watched it unfold.

It was enough to leave two brothers from North Carolina, Joe and Jeff Bostic, in complete awe of a rivalry they did not know or understand when they joined the Tigers in the mid-1970s. Both established themselves as elite college offensive linemen, and both went on to long and successful careers in the NFL. But the Clemson-Carolina rivalry stuck with them and still does to this day.

Joe Bostic was junior offensive lineman on the 1977 Clemson team that rose from the ashes of a three-win season in 1976 to win eight games and finish second in the ACC. *Courtesy of Clemson University Sports Information Department.*

"When I got down there, people would always say, 'We've got to beat Carolina,'" Joe Bostic said. "But in my mind, I'm thinking we'd already played North Carolina."

LITTLE WAS EXPECTED OF Clemson entering the 1977 season. Red Parker had been fired after losing fifteen games in 1975 and 1976, and not much was known about the man who replaced him. Parker hired Charley Pell from Virginia Tech in 1976 to be the Tigers' defensive coordinator, and Pell was elevated to head coach immediately after Parker's ouster. Pell scrapped Parker's veer offense and went with a Power I that theoretically would expand opportunities to pass the ball to Butler, the most talented and athletic player on the team.

Steve Kenney, a junior offensive lineman on the 1977 team, recalls Pell as a likable figure amongst the players. Pell played for Bear Bryant's first national title team at Alabama in 1961, and his chief objective at Clemson was teaching the Tigers how to win.

"There was something different about Coach Pell," Kenney said.

> *Some coaches will take it easy on you in practice and be a players' coach; some will be relentless and dog you and tell you how sorry you are. Pell worked you really hard and was really tough on you, but when practice was over he expected you to get first-class treatment. When we had a victory, he wanted us to feel like we were world champions. He didn't want us to be surprised to win. He wanted us to expect to win. He wanted us to be cocky.*

Coming off 2-9 and 3-6-2 seasons, there wasn't much for the Tigers to feel cocky about in the summer of 1977. Parker had quietly stockpiled an impressive array of talent in his 1975 and 1976 recruiting classes, collecting a large number of players who would end up in the NFL, but the pundits weren't impressed. The *Journal* of Atlanta called Clemson "a severe depression in the geography of ACC football." The newspapers in South Carolina weren't particularly glowing, either; the Tigers were given almost no chance to finish above .500 overall, and the consensus was a fifth-place ACC finish.

Clemson closed the 1976 season with a 28–9 upset of Carolina at Death Valley, denying the Gamecocks a spot in a bowl. Fuller was returning for his junior season, and as Pell's first game approached, he told a gathering of ACC writers that Fuller would be the best quarterback in the conference in 1977. The prediction elicited chuckles from scribes who had watched the Tigers win just two of ten conference games in Fuller's freshman and sophomore seasons.

FROM THE ACC'S INCEPTION in 1953 to 1967, Clemson won or shared six conference titles under Frank Howard. But the program slipped over the next nine seasons, producing just one winning record as North Carolina and Maryland became the conference's power teams.

Maryland, which had won three consecutive ACC titles, had little apparent respect for Clemson entering the 1977 season opener between the two schools. The Terrapins' quarterback was quoted as saying he couldn't wait to face the Tigers' defense after spending August laboring against his own.

Clemson put forth a respectable showing in the opener against the number ten Terrapins, who had beaten the Tigers five straight years. Maryland made it six in a row that day in Death Valley, but Pell's team was encouraging in a 21–14 defeat.

Seven days later, Clemson ventured to Georgia. The Tigers hadn't won in Athens since 1914, and Georgia had champagne ready in anticipation of coach Vince Dooley's 100th victory. Clemson ruined the party with an emotional 7–6 win that provoked Pell to stop the team buses at a convenience store on the trip back to Clemson. The coach bought cigars for everyone, and the team triumphantly puffed all the way home.

The Tigers became hooked. Pell bought another round of cigars the next week after a 31–14 smoking of Georgia Tech in Atlanta, and the habit continued through a magical seven-game winning streak that put Clemson in the national polls for the first time since 1959. The Tigers would win eleven games in 1978, eight in 1979 and then the national title in 1981. But at this point the Tigers were breaking new ground, and it was intoxicating to a team and fans who'd known little more than struggles for the longest time.

"We'd see the headlines in the newspapers: 'Charley's angels win again,'" Kenney remembered. "We won big the next year, but in 1977 it was all new to us."

THE GAMECOCKS CONSIDERED THEMSELVES the superior program entering that season, the third under coach Jim Carlen. The off-season was not easy after the unexpected loss to a three-win Clemson team. But the Gamecocks were still drawing comfort and satisfaction from a 56–20 massacre of the Tigers in 1975, and two freshman running backs named George Rogers and Johnnie Wright created optimism in Columbia.

Carolina began the season with an impressive 4-1 record, the only blemish a two-point home loss to Georgia. But everything turned when

Duke surmounted a 21–3 deficit in Columbia and handed the Gamecocks a deflating 25–21 defeat. Carolina entered the November 19 finale against Clemson having lost four of five games, and Carlen was sniping at the press for giving up on his team.

Though assured of a banner year, and one win away from its first eight-win season in eighteen years, Clemson was a frustrated team as it began preparing for the Gamecocks. A missed extra point was costly in a 13–13 tie at North Carolina, a result that snapped the seven-game winning streak and cost the Tigers their first ACC championship since 1967.

An even bigger gut punch came a week before the game in Columbia. Notre Dame brought a number five ranking and a quarterback named Joe Montana to an electric setting in Clemson, and the Tigers built a 17–7 lead that had the overflow crowd of more than fifty-four thousand on the edge of delirium. Clemson had opportunities to extend the lead even further but squandered them by losing two fumbles deep in Irish territory. Notre Dame capitalized on two more turnovers with a pair of fourth-quarter touchdown runs by Montana and won 21–17. The Irish later finished the season number one.

Notre Dame coach Dan Devine said after the game that Clemson had better talent than Southern Cal, a Top 10 team the Irish had dispatched with ease earlier in the season. "Their team should be undefeated," he said.

Montana was just as impressed. "Clemson is quick and tough," he told reporters. "I expected a tough game and that's just what we got. I know a couple of guys who play at North Carolina and North Carolina State and they had told me Clemson was one of the toughest places to play in the country. They were right."

The Tigers were not consoled by the favorable reviews. In their minds, they'd given away two games against great teams. Senior linebacker Mark Heniford said after the game that coming close against a national power "doesn't do a thing for me."

"Sure," he said, "I take some pride in the fact that we played that well against what many people consider the number one team in the nation. But damn playing good. We're out there to win. And we should have won."

Clemson was faced with the difficult task of getting its emotions in order for another big game that became even bigger when ABC announced plans to regionally televise the clash in Columbia. It was to be the first live telecast ever of the rivalry, and kickoff was moved from 1:30 to 4:10 p.m. to accommodate.

A State of Disunion

PELL SEEMED UNEASY EARLY in the week, knowing his team had to recover from two draining and unrewarding games. Carolina had an open date before the previous week's win over Wake Forest, and Pell said the Gamecocks "didn't even have to open their playbook" against the Demon Deacons.

"They didn't throw a pass the entire second half. We threw the index, the table of contents and everything else against Notre Dame."

Pell had experienced the rivalry just once, the 1976 upset in Parker's last game as head coach, but already he seemed to have a full appreciation of its importance and impact in the Palmetto State. The Tigers had their sights set on a big bowl game, but Pell said the rivalry game "decides who walks down the street as state champion and who hides in a closet for a year."

Clemson's fans were distracted by the hope of their team's first bowl appearance in almost two decades. A date in the Gator Bowl had not yet been made official, but the orange-clad masses were already booking their flights to Jacksonville, chartering buses, making hotel reservations and gobbling up tickets as the Carolina game approached.

Carlen, whose team entered at 5-5 with no hope of a bowl appearance, knew he was facing a daunting task against a talented team. He told reporters that Clemson was the best opponent Carolina would face all season.

"They're a lot like North Carolina," a team that beat the Gamecocks handily earlier in the year. "But the difference is Fuller and Butler, and that's a big difference...They can hurt you with a number of receivers. But Butler is the one who drowns you."

The Gamecocks were on their last breath in the third quarter. Clemson had entered halftime up 17–0, then Ken Callicutt burst fifty-two yards for a touchdown to spark celebration and relaxation on the Tigers' sideline. Carolina posed almost no threat to surmount the twenty-four-point deficit because the Gamecocks spent the first half using two tight ends and running the ball.

As a junior receiver in 1977, Jerry Butler caught forty-seven passes for 824 yards while averaging 17.5 yards per catch. *Courtesy of Clemson University Sports Information Department.*

Pell spent the week telling his players that the Tigers needed to beat the Gamecocks to ensure a trip to the Gator Bowl, but athletics director Bill McLellan revealed to reporters before the game that Clemson was headed to Jacksonville win or lose. Pell made the decision to keep the news from the team until after the game, and the motivational ploy seemed to be working marvelously.

The Gamecocks' starting defensive players provided more motivation by taping individual mug shots of their counterparts on the front of their helmets. Joe Bostic, a right guard, remembers being dumbfounded early in the game when he looked across the line and saw his own picture staring at him from linebacker David Prezioso's helmet. Said Kenney, the left guard, "I remember thinking: 'What a bunch of dorks.'"

The Tigers also still remembered what had happened two years earlier in Columbia. Joe Bostic was a freshman on the 1975 team that had absorbed what remains Clemson's worst loss in the rivalry—thirty-six points.

"I remember going to visit my uncle in Chester after that game, and people were mocking us and laughing at us and everything else," he said. "They just kicked our ass up one side and down the other. A lot of guys on the team said, 'We're not losing to these guys again.'"

THE PERVERSE PLEASURE OF returning the favor gave way to some nervousness as the Gamecocks scored two quick touchdowns, the first a seventy-seven-yard run by Spencer Clark on an option pitch. Then, Clemson fans began to panic.

Carolina pulled within 24–20 with 7:02 on the clock. Five minutes later, the Gamecocks converted a miraculous fourth and ten when Ron Bass found receiver Phil Logan on a curl route down the right seam. The throw was high, but Logan leaped and snared it. He had a first down, and he ended up getting much more after several Tigers collided. Logan used a couple of good blocks and crossed over to the left side before skittering into the end zone for a forty-yard catch-and-run that put the Gamecocks up.

"You really couldn't hear any South Carolina fans when it was 24–0," said Jeff Bostic, a sophomore center on that team. "But when it got to be 27–24, that was a different stadium."

In the chaos of Carolina's unthinkable comeback, Joe Bostic remembers confronting senior right tackle Lacy Brumley on the sideline. Brumley had suffered an injury earlier in the game and was declared unfit to return by head trainer Fred Hoover.

Bostic: "Brumley, you need to get your ass on the field."

Brumley: "I can't; Hoover has taken my knee pads."

Bostic: "Go get one of the freshmen and tell them to give you their damn knee pads."

Brumley obliged, stuffing a freshman's pads into his pants. He walked up to his backup and told him to sit down, that he was going to play the rest of the game.

There was plenty of reason for Clemson's offense to think the worst as it huddled during a TV timeout with 1:39 remaining, needing sixty-seven yards for victory. The Tigers had squandered all those opportunities the previous two weeks against North Carolina and Notre Dame, and now they were imploding in spectacular fashion. On the Gamecocks sideline, players were lifting up their jerseys to reveal T-shirts that read "No Cigar Today." Carolina defensive coordinator Richard Bell came up with the idea for the shirts that mocked Clemson's new postgame tradition.

And that's about when Joe Bostic started to lose his lunch.

"It was just terrible," he said. "When you're ahead 24–0 with less than a half of football to play, there's no way you should be behind at all. We had a good defense that year. There was no damn way anybody should score four touchdowns on our defense in less than a half. Just no way."

THE QUEASY MOMENTS WERE brief because everyone remembers Fuller injecting the huddle with calmness and confidence.

"He said: 'We're going down the field and scoring a damn touchdown and winning the damn game,'" Joe Bostic remembers. "Fuller was talented, but he was a great leader. He was just one of those guys who'd say things, and you just thought, 'By God, he'll figure out a way to do it.' And most of the time, he did."

Kenney's recollection of Fuller's words was: "Give me a little protection, and we'll go down and score and get the hell out of here."

After minimal gains on first and second downs, Clemson faced a third and seven. Joe Bostic looked Fuller in the eyes and said: "Now would be a good time to make a big play." Fuller's response: "We've got them right where we want them. Just give me a little bit of time."

The big play came when Fuller found Rick Weddington for a twenty-six-yard gain to the Carolina thirty-eight. After spiking the ball to stop the clock, Fuller hit Dwight Clark for an eighteen-yard pickup to the twenty. Fuller later said these two plays, which sent four receivers downfield and allowed Fuller to take his pick, were the Tigers' best of the year. The offensive line gave him the time he needed on both plays.

Clemson was in its two-minute offense, and Pell later said the Tigers called a pass play to the sidelines to stop the clock. Lined up on the left side, Jerry Butler was to make a "seven cut," a corner route to the left sideline. He had the option to change his route if he faced pressure from the outside by the defensive back covering him.

On the Gamecock sideline, coaches didn't have enough time to call another defense. Thus the eleven players on the field were supposed to remain in the defense deployed on the previous play.

"One of our defensive backs didn't remember that," Carlen said after the game. "Everybody played it right but one fellow."

The cornerback in front of Butler cut off the planned sideline route. Butler ran down the seam, gave a head fake to the middle and looked back to see Fuller facing mild pressure after he dropped back and rolled to his left. Butler knew Fuller wouldn't take a sack in that situation, that he'd been taught to throw the ball away upon facing pressure.

Fuller unleashed a pass toward the back of the end zone, and Butler figured it was a throwaway. Initially, he didn't think the ball was catchable. But he went after it and...

"I couldn't see it," said Jeff Bostic. "You don't have a lot of great views from where I was. But you can normally tell from the crowd noise. When the visiting team is in the stadium and you just hear a mild roar coming from one area, you know your team has just done something good."

Decades later, Butler would reveal that he had two jammed fingers in his left hand. He'd created his own homemade wrap that allowed him to spread the fingers apart, and he credited the contraption with allowing him to come down with the ball that night.

"Jerry was such a great athlete," said Joe Bostic. "He was the best football player on our team. He was a world-class sprinter, had tremendous athletic ability. You could see it in that picture: He can jump out of the damn sky."

In the press box at Williams-Brice Stadium, a photographer from *The State* named Larry Cagle was using a newfangled motor-drive camera to take pictures in sequence. He managed to capture Butler's catch in perhaps the most defining photo of the rivalry's history.

Steve Fuller and Jerry Butler are responsible for perhaps the most famous play in the history of the Clemson-Carolina football rivalry. *Courtesy of Clemson University Sports Information Department.*

After the game, a despondent Carlen said all the athletic ability in the world wouldn't have mattered had all eleven Gamecocks played the right defense.

"One defensive back didn't remember which defense we ran the previous play and blew the coverage," he said. "There's no point in in-pointing him, but I think we would have made the play if he had been in the defense we had going. We had the pass coverage where the ball was."

There was still time for Carolina to answer, and the Gamecocks had the ball at midfield after a personal-foul penalty on the extra point. Heniford, the senior linebacker, jubilantly greeted Fuller on the sideline after the dramatic touchdown. Fuller's response: "You think you idiots on defense can hold them now?"

The defense held, and Clemson walked away from a classic game with a classic victory. John Lanahan, chairman of the Gator Bowl committee, made an appearance in Clemson's locker room after the game.

"I'd heard a lot about this series, but I didn't believe a damned thing I'd heard before tonight!" he yelled. Pell told the press that it was "the most exciting closing minutes of any I can remember since I've been in football."

After almost two decades of obscurity, Clemson went on to reassert itself as a power by winning the 1981 national title and claiming seven ACC championships from 1978 to 1991. A young offensive line coach named Danny Ford would take over late the next season after Pell's abrupt departure for Florida, and the Tigers ended up compiling a 12-3-1 record over the Gamecocks from 1976 to 1991.

Late on that night in 1977, the participants walked away knowing they'd been a part of something special. The winners walked away through a haze of cigar smoke.

Said Joe Bostic, "That's a game you can kind of hang your hat on for years and years and years."

Clemson coach Tommy Bowden is carried by his players after the Tigers' 63–17 dismantling of the Gamecocks in 2003. *Courtesy of Clemson University Sports Information Department.*

The scoreboard after the 1998 game—the last for Clemson's Tommy West and Carolina's Brad Scott as head coaches of their respective teams. *Courtesy of Clemson University Sports Information Department.*

Clemson defensive back Crezdon Butler grabs the facemask of Carolina receiver Chris Culliver in the 2007 game. *Courtesy of Clemson University Sports Information Department.*

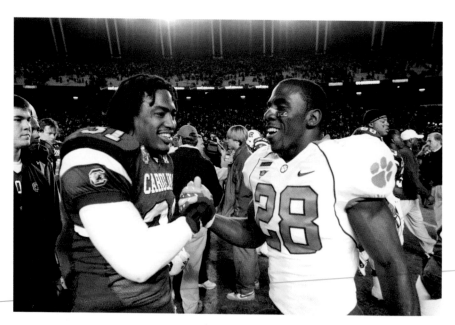

Carolina's Gerrod Sinclair and Clemson's C.J. Spiller share a laugh after the Tigers' narrow victory in 2007. *Courtesy of Clemson University Sports Information Department.*

Clemson quarterback Charlie Whitehurst is jubilant after securing the first down that sealed a 13–9 win in Columbia in 2005, his senior season. *Courtesy of Clemson University Sports Information Department.*

Lou Holtz and Tommy Bowden share a laugh before the 2003 game in Columbia. Bowden entered the game facing speculation about his job security. *Courtesy of Clemson University Sports Information Department.*

James Davis bulls toward the end zone on a pivotal drive in the 2005 game. *Courtesy of Clemson University Sports Information Department.*

Clemson quarterback Kyle Parker escapes pressure in the 2009 game. The Gamecocks won 34–17, bringing the Tigers back down to earth after they wrapped up the Atlantic Division title a week earlier. *Courtesy of Zachary Hanby.*

Cullen Harper celebrates Mark Buchholz's buzzer-beating field goal after Harper led the Tigers on a frantic drive in the final moments of the 2007 game. *Courtesy of Clemson University Sports Information Department.*

A creation at Clemson's 1971 homecoming game against Wake Forest chides Carolina's exit from the ACC. *Courtesy of James Stepp.*

Left: Clemson assistant Chris Rumph, who played at South Carolina in the 1990s, makes his first visit back to Williams-Brice Stadium in 2007 as a member of the Tigers' staff. *Courtesy of Clemson University Sports Information Department.*

Below: View from the top of Williams-Brice stadium during the 2009 game in Columbia. *Courtesy of Paul Collins, Gamecock Central.*

Carolina receiver Tori Gurley hauls in a deep ball and fights for extra yardage in the 2009 game. *Courtesy of Paul Collins, Gamecock Central.*

George Rogers runs against Clemson in Columbia. Rogers, who won the Heisman Trophy in 1980, never reached the end zone against the Tigers and lost three of four in the rivalry game. *Courtesy of the University of South Carolina Archives, South Caroliniana Library.*

Freshman "Rats" at Clemson stand guard over Thomas Green Clemson's statue. It was common in the 1940s, '50s and '60s for students at each school to raid the opposing campus and vandalize monuments. *Courtesy of James Stepp.*

Wide-angle view of Death Valley during the 2008 game. The Tigers won 31–14, and a day later the interim tag was stripped from Dabo Swinney's title. Swinney had stepped in for Tommy Bowden halfway through the season after Bowden stepped down. *Courtesy of Zachary Hanby.*

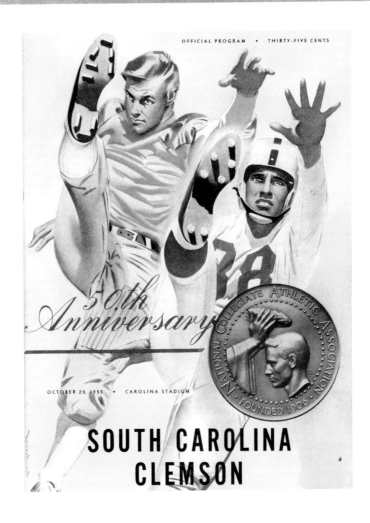

EAST STAND
GATE NO. **11**

Sec. **48**

17

Row

N° Seat **12**

VOID IF DETACHED—NOT REDEEMABLE

Univ. of S. C.
1955
versus
Clemson

Thursday, Oct. 20, 1955

ADMISSION - $4.80

2:00
P.M.

THE STATE COMMERCIAL PRINTING CO.

EAST STAND

GATE NO. **11**

SEC. **47**

ROW **12**

SEAT **15**

ADMISSION $5.00
STATE TAX .50
STAD. BOND FEE .25
TOTAL $5.75

The Final Curtain...

UNIV. of S. C.
versus
CLEMSON

BIG THURSDAY
OCT. 22, 1959
2:00 P.M.

U. S. C. RESERVES THE RIGHT TO REFUND AND NOT ADMIT TO STADIUM • VOID IF DETA

WEST STAND

3
GATE

14
SEC.

20
ROW

12
SEAT

SOUTH CAROLINA vs. CLEMSON

Adm. 5.00
S. Tax .50 $5.75
S.Bd.Fee .25

1965 • CAROLINA STADIUM • 1965

So. Car. vs Clemson

CAROLINA STADIUM
Join the Gamecock Club
No Refund S. Tax
Adm. 5.00
S. Tax .50 $5.75
Sta.Bd.Fee .25

NOV.
20
2 P.M.

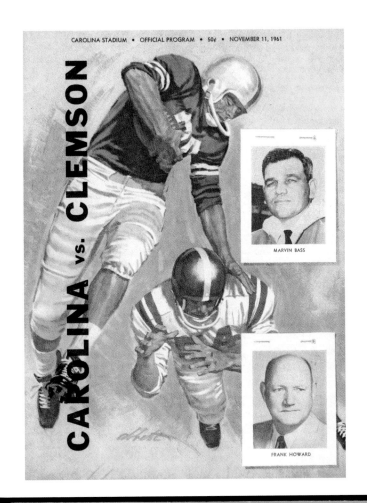

CAROLINA vs. CLEMSON

MARVIN BASS

FRANK HOWARD

FOOTBALL

FIGHTING

1981

GAMECOCKS

WILLIAMS-BRICE STADIUM
Columbia, S. C.

SOUTH
CAROLINA
VS.
CLEMSON
—
SATURDAY
NOV. 21, 1981

NO REFUND

JOIN THE
GAMECOCK
CLUB

WEST STAND
UPPER LEVEL

Sec. **304**

Row 27

Seat 23

Adm. 9.00
S.B.F. 1.00 $10.00
Incl. Adm. Tax

CLEMSON

WE WILL HAVE **CHICKEN AND DUMPLINGS** WHEN HE COMES...

CLEMSON SOUTH CAROLINA

CLEMSON MEMORIAL STADIUM NOV. 12, 1960

GAMECOCKS

OFFICIAL PROGRAM 50¢

DAD'S DAY

SOUTH CAROLINA

SATURDAY
November 18, 2000

$32.00

NORTH STANDS

5 — GATE · L — SEC. · O — ROW · 24 — SEAT

CLEMSON FOOTBALL

HISTORICAL SOUVENIR PROGRAM

BIG THURSDAY

1896 - 1959

UNIVERSITY OF SOUTH CAROLINA
VS
CLEMSON COLLEGE

CAROLINA STADIUM COLUMBIA, S.C.
OCTOBER 22, 1959 - PRICE ONE DOLLAR

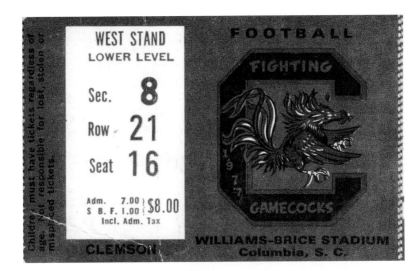

WEST STAND
LOWER LEVEL

Sec. **8**

Row **21**

Seat **16**

Adm. 7.00
S.B.F. 1.00 } $8.00
Incl. Adm. Tax

CLEMSON

FOOTBALL

FIGHTING

1977

GAMECOCKS

WILLIAMS-BRICE STADIUM
Columbia, S. C.

SOUTH
CAROLINA
CLEMSON

CAROLINA STADIUM
NOV. 20, 1965
OFFICIAL PROGRAM 50c

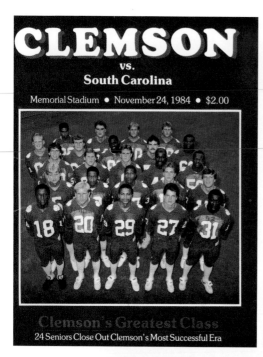

CLEMSON
vs.
South Carolina

Memorial Stadium ● November 24, 1984 ● $2.00

Clemson's Greatest Class
24 Seniors Close Out Clemson's Most Successful Era

National Football Champions

THE HILL

CLEMSON vs. SOUTH CAROLINA
"GO TIGERS"
SAT., NOV. 19, 1988 - TBA

WEST STAND

11	X	0	3
GATE	SEC.	ROW	SEAT

SOUTH CAROLINA

GATE	SEC.	ROW	SEAT
	1	46	20

WEST LOWER

JEFF GRANTZ · GARRY MOTT

SOUTH 1975 CAROLINA vs. CLEMSON
A Commitment to Excellence
Academics & Athletics

2 0 0 6   T I G E R   F O O T B A L L

November 25, 2006 • Clemson Memorial Stadium • ClemsonTigers.com

Clemson

40
Anthony
WATERS

93
Gaines
ADAMS

80
Tramaine
BILLIE

Death Valley
DEFENSE

solid
ORANGE

VERSUS South Carolina

NORTH STAND

Enter Gate **13**

Sec. **64**

Row **24**

Seat **15**
CLEMSON

Adm.   5.00
St. Tax   .50 $5.75
Sta.Bd.Fee.25

U. S. C. vs. Clemson

SATURDAY
NOV. 11
1961

KICK-OFF
2:00 P. M.

HOLD YOUR
OWN TICKET

U.S.C. Reserves the Right to Refund and Not Admit to Stadium
VOID IF DETACHED -:- NOT REDEEMABLE

WELDON, WILLIAMS & LICK, FT.SMITH, ARK.

CAROLINA CLEMSON

SENIOR SECONDARY

Norris Brown

Eric Geter

James Trapp

Clemson
Memorial Stadium vs. November 21, 1992
South Carolina

Robert O'Neal
Always All ACC

14

A FASHION STATEMENT

1980

A BOUT HALFWAY THROUGH THE 1980 season, Len Gough gave Danny Ford a call and asked him to come to the equipment room.

Gough was a 1974 Clemson graduate who became the football team's equipment manager in 1976. He was more of an idea guy than anything else, and he'd thought of something that might inject some life into a team struggling through a difficult season. A pair of orange football pants had sat inside Gough's desk for years, collecting dust.

"I always thought it might be neat to do something different with orange pants," Gough remembered. "We were looking for some kind of spark, some kind of energy."

Generally, color combinations in uniforms were basic and conservative in those days. Home games called for solid-color jerseys and white pants. So when Gough asked Ford what he thought about the Tigers wearing all orange for a home game, it was an unconventional idea.

FORD WAS ONLY A year away from ushering Clemson's program to a national title, and the Tigers later spent decades unsuccessfully trying to taste the glory Ford delivered in the 1980s. But at this time, Ford was not yet known as a great coach or anything close to it. He was merely a young, inexperienced former offensive line coach who was trying to win over a fan base that had its doubts about the man who replaced Charley Pell in late 1978.

Quarterback Homer Jordan, wearing all orange, tries to elude pressure in the 1980 game against Carolina. *Courtesy of Clemson University Sports Information Department.*

An eight-win season in 1979 closed in sour fashion after a 13–9 loss at South Carolina and a narrow Peach Bowl defeat to Baylor. After a 4-1 start in 1980, the Tigers suffered a 34–17 home shellacking at the hands of a Duke team that would finish 2-9. The next week, a loss at North Carolina State left fans grumbling about the thirty-two-year-old coach from Alabama who chewed tobacco and spoke with a pronounced drawl.

The offense, which lost a number of key players from the previous year, made self-impaling mistakes. Ford faced criticism for sticking with sophomore quarterback Homer Jordan. There was no senior starter on offense, and the starting offense and defense featured five freshmen and four sophomores.

In Columbia, the Gamecocks appeared to be growing into a power in the sixth year under coach Jim Carlen. They were loaded with NFL prospects entering the season. The emotional victory over Clemson a year earlier had given the program eight wins over college competition for the first time in school history. The Gamecocks went to number four Southern Cal for the third game of the season and walked away with some respect in a 23–13 loss. A week later, they went to Michigan and pulled off a momentous 17–14 upset of a Wolverine team that would finish undefeated in the Big Ten and win the Rose Bowl.

Senior running back George Rogers was vaulting to the top of Heisman lists with a powerful, punishing running style. The Gamecocks rose to number fourteen in the rankings after a 6-1 start, heading into a mammoth showdown in Athens against a fourth-ranked Georgia team led by spectacular freshman running back Herschel Walker. The game was televised nationally by ABC, Keith Jackson handling play-by-play duties. A late Rogers fumble deep in enemy territory allowed Georgia to preserve a 13–10 victory, and the Bulldogs marched on to the national title.

A WEEK BEFORE THE regular-season finale in Clemson, neither the Gamecocks nor the Tigers gave their fans much reason for excitement. Clemson went to Maryland and suffered a 34–7 pounding against a good Terrapins team, ending the Tigers' hopes of landing in the Peach Bowl. The Gamecocks needed a miraculous, sixty-two-yard touchdown pass with fifty-seven seconds left to beat Wake Forest 39–38 before a rain-soaked crowd in Columbia.

In his final home game, Carolina quarterback Garry Harper was close to tears after hearing a fan berate him in response to a late interception. "Hey Harper, I'm glad you're a senior!" came the barb, directed at the quarterback who had helped lead the Gamecocks to back-to-back eight-win seasons.

The day after watching his defense surrender 447 yards, Carlen tore into his team during a Sunday meeting. He also made the decision to close practices to the media during Clemson week.

"The players were stunned in yesterday's meeting," Carlen said during his Monday press conference. "I guess they thought it was the first time an 8-2 team had ever been chewed out."

The Gamecocks were ranked fourteenth nationally and were eight-point favorites. The *News and Courier* of Charleston posted predictions for the game from its twelve sports staffers, and eleven of them picked Carolina. Carlen, though, expressed concern that Clemson would pull off an ambush similar to 1976, when a young but talented Tigers team entered the game with two wins but blasted the Gamecocks 28–9 to set up banner seasons in 1977 and 1978.

In Clemson, Ford and his assistants weren't experiencing much comfort as they tried to turn away from the Maryland beating and shift their focus to the visit from the Gamecocks. A lengthy injury list, plus an unusually large number of assorted nicks and bruises, convinced Ford that the Tigers would not be able to do any hitting all week. Ford said that eleven of his defensive players were afflicted with some type of injury. Included were starting defensive backs Terry Kinard and Eddie Geathers, who missed the Maryland game and were not expected to play in the finale.

"I don't see any way that we can afford to work in pads this week," the coach told reporters. "Our coaches want the players to put on shorts and pads for some sled work. I told them that if I see anybody hit anything other than a sled, the pads come off for the rest of the week. We're thinner than thin right now. The most important person on our staff this week is Fred Hoover, our head trainer. A lot about how we play Saturday will be determined by who we can get well by then."

IN CLEMSON'S EQUIPMENT ROOM, Len Gough was getting apprehensive. The order for one hundred pairs of bright orange pants had been made weeks earlier, but getting the garb to Clemson was not an easy process. The pants were being produced at Russell Athletic's plant in Alexander City, Alabama, but they would not be ready until Friday—less than twenty-four hours before the Tigers were to take the field for the 1:00 p.m. game at Memorial Stadium.

The operation was still top secret. Gough estimates that a total of six people knew of it at this point. Even the Russell Athletic representative who handled the order was sworn to secrecy.

On Friday, Gough was on the university plane bound for Alabama. The only other person on board was assistant athletics director and ticket manager Earl Ambrose, who was also a retired air force colonel and

Len Gough, the former equipment manager who helped conceive and devise the top-secret plan to unveil the orange pants for the Carolina game. *Courtesy of Clemson University Sports Information Department.*

at the time served as the school's pilot. To make room for the precious cargo, Ambrose and Gough removed the seats from the plane before the plane departed the Clemson area.

"You'd be surprised how much room a bunch of boxes of pants takes up," Gough said.

The pickup in Alabama went as planned, and by Friday night Gough was pulling into a parking space at the team's hotel in Anderson. Riding shotgun was a sealed box containing one pair of the orange pants. Ford secretly showed them to the team's seniors that night, but the grand unveiling was to take place the next morning before the team breakfast.

Earlier in the day on Friday, Clemson's training staff had been setting up the locker room at Memorial Stadium as the Gamecocks went through their walk-through on the field. Chip Winchester, then a sophomore student trainer for the Tigers, remembers Carolina's training staff barging into the locker room and demanding to see Clemson's new purple jerseys.

"They told us the rumor around Columbia all week was that we were going to wear purple jerseys," Winchester said. "We assured them we weren't, and our managers even showed them that the lockers had already been set up with orange jerseys and white pants. We didn't even know about the orange pants at the time."

FORD BECAME KNOWN AS a master motivator while leading the Tigers to greatness during the 1980s, and he skillfully choreographed this fashion statement to create maximum impact on team and fans alike.

The rumors about Ford's departure intensified in the wake of the shellacking at Maryland. It didn't help that most Clemson fans were chalking up a loss to a favored Gamecocks team led by a player, Rogers, who'd established himself as the frontrunner for the Heisman Trophy.

Ford produced a dramatic Gator Bowl win over Ohio State in his first game as coach. He won eight games in 1979. But the program appeared to have slipped since the magical run in 1977 and 1978 under Pell, who left a Top 10 program for Florida after the 1978 regular season.

A loss to Carolina would have assured Clemson its first losing season since 1976, and it was hard for Tigers fans to see success on the horizon despite a number of close losses by the young 1980 team. Not many fans wanted to hear about the injuries or the key pieces Ford lost from his 1979 team—his quarterback, his top two running backs, his starting center and both starting guards.

Chuck Reedy, then in his third year coaching the Tigers' running backs, said the assistant coaches spent most of the season worrying that it would be their last in Clemson. The week of the game against Carolina, the administration assured Ford that his job was not in danger. But that didn't eliminate the apprehension.

Head coach Danny Ford meets with his staff. *Courtesy of Special Collections, Clemson University Libraries*

"Danny's job was in jeopardy," Reedy said. "We were very much afraid that Danny was not going to make it. He had been there two years, and we were 8-4 and then looking at 5-6. It was a year of a lot of discontent... If we'd have gone out there and gotten the hell beat out of us by South Carolina, there would have been no guarantee that would have held up. If enough people with money came in and said, 'He's got to go,' we would have been done."

The chatter and the speculation during game week became so pervasive and annoying to Ford that he issued a statement Friday night denying he would resign after the game.

THE NEXT DAY, THE team gathered for its morning breakfast at the Holiday Inn. Billy Davis, a freshman defensive back on the 1980 team, remembers tension that was typical on game days. "There's just nothing that resembles a pre-game meal in football," Davis said. "Everybody is talking low, and you don't eat much. You feel like you're going to toss your cookies half the time."

Suddenly, Ford amplified the tension to a heart-pounding level when he stood up and began to speak. "I have something to say," he said, "and you all ought to be the first to know."

Ford's players had heard the rumors. They thought their coach was about to confirm them. They thought he was about to announce his resignation. "You should have seen it," Ford would say a day later. "All of their eyes got big as saucers."

Ford then grabbed a box from the floor and placed it on the table. He pulled out the pair of orange pants and said, "We're going to wear these today."

Immediately, the tension and the drama and the suspense yielded to screams of relief and the unexpected joy of doing something new and exciting. The power of the moment still gives chills not only to those who experienced it but also to plenty who merely heard about it.

"I don't know if you've ever been in a room where you could literally feel the electricity," said Reedy, who was with Ford for his entire Clemson coaching tenure. "I mean, it was instant. There was just a damn rush of emotion."

Said Billy Davis:

> The whole place just erupted. I remember everyone standing up and jumping up and down. Things just hadn't gone right for us that year, but Coach Ford was the master of the mind games and the motivation. It was like we were pulling off a secret mission or something. To this day, I still get goose bumps thinking about that bus ride from Anderson to Clemson. We were just super excited that this was the Carolina game. We're eighteen-, nineteen- and twenty-year-old kids, and we're going to do something we'd never done.

THE NEXT OBJECTIVE WAS to spring the surprise on a stadium full of fans. Per Ford's plan, the team would dress in the typical white pants when it arrived at Memorial Stadium. The thigh pads, knee pads and hip pads had already been placed in the orange pants that hung in the players' lockers, but the Tigers would go out for pre-game warm-ups wearing the pad-less white pants and orange jerseys.

Once back in the locker room, the team hastily removed the white pants and went all orange for the first time. Ford had to send someone out for the coin toss, and he had a plan for that: Geathers, the injured cornerback, was designated the game captain and strolled to the middle of the field wearing a game jersey and jeans.

The team still had to board the buses for the ride around the stadium to the Hill, and it was a given that some fans in the southwest corner of the stadium would notice the new look as the team walked from the locker room to the buses behind the west end zone. Gough tried to build a "people wall" from the locker room to the buses, lining up managers and trainers in an effort to shield the orange pants from fans.

Bubba Diggs was a tight end for the Tigers at the time, and he was sitting out the 1980 season with an injury after playing in 1978 and 1979. He didn't accompany the team on the buses for the trip to the Hill, instead taking a slow walk from the locker room to the Tigers' sideline on the south side of the stadium.

"People around the end zone saw the orange pants," Diggs said. "The crowd in that section erupted and went crazy, and then the crowd in the next section erupted and went crazy. It was almost like doing the wave; the word was spreading and the crowd got louder and louder. I was on the sideline watching it all happen. And when the buses opened up on the other side and everybody saw the guys get off the bus with those orange pants on, you couldn't hear yourself think. It was unbelievable."

CLEMSON KEPT THE GAME close through the first half, and the score was tied 6–6 late in the third quarter when the Gamecocks seemed poised for a momentum-grabbing score. On second and ten from the Clemson sixteen, Carlen decided to try a pass instead of sticking with a successful running game. The decision backfired when Harper misfired on a pass that was intercepted by Underwood and taken sixty-four yards the other way to set up a Clemson touchdown. On the Gamecocks' next possession, Underwood picked off another errant Harper throw and returned it thirty-seven yards to the end zone to put Clemson up 21–6.

Later, after the game, Harper began crying when a reporter asked him if he thought about the first interception as he began to make the second throw that Underwood intercepted.

Underwood was a veteran leader for the Tigers, and he ended up totaling 170 career tackles. But until November 22, 1980, he had not managed to snare an interception. And he might've considered himself lucky to play in this game after suffering painful back spasms earlier in the week. Hoover, the longtime trainer, fitted Underwood with a portable electronic muscle stimulator that he wore under his jersey during the game to ease the pain.

Clemson won 27–6, achieving its largest margin of victory over Carolina in fourteen years and permanently tarnishing an otherwise successful season by the Gamecocks. Carlen was crestfallen after the game, accepting blame for passing the ball when the run was working.

"I'm about as disappointed and low as a person can get," the coach said.

Reedy is still dumbfounded that Carlen even thought of going away from Rogers, who finished with 168 yards on twenty-eight carries.

"They were by far the superior football team. I mean, it wasn't even close. There was no comparison between the two football teams. They would hand the ball to George Rogers, hand the ball to George Rogers, pitch it to George Rogers, and we couldn't stop them. We would have never stopped them."

Rogers won the Heisman Trophy soon thereafter, but he never scored a touchdown against the Tigers. It was the same fate that befell Georgia's Walker in his three meetings with Clemson from 1980 to 1982. Giddy Clemson fans left the stadium chanting, "George who?" Before he boarded a bus for the trip back to Columbia, Rogers vented to reporters about what he considered dirty play by Clemson's defense:

> Once they tackle you, they try to twist and turn your legs around and hurt you. If we could play like that, it might have been even. But Coach Carlen won't let us play that way. I don't like a team that keeps talking to you like Clemson does. When you've got a bunch of big mouths like they have, it takes away from the fun of playing. They try to tear your knees up. They're bad players. They don't show no sportsmanship out there.

Also after the game, Gamecocks middle guard Emanuel Weaver was asked about the orange pants and their effect on the outcome. "No way. Pants don't play the game. I don't even see why they wore those stupid pants."

Clemson defensive tackle Steve Durham told reporters that he hoped the Tigers didn't hurt Rogers's chances of winning the Heisman: "He's a good one, and no one else deserves it more. Coach Ford told us he was going to fire us up; he said we'd warm up in white pants and then switch to the orange ones and that the change would shock them. He said that would be the first shock, and the second shock would be when we'd stop Rogers and Carolina."

FORD WAS UNCHARACTERISTICALLY JUBILANT in the locker room immediately after the game. He jumped onto a table and danced as the room chanted, "Cockadoodle loo, cockadoodle loo, Carolina Gamecocks to hell with you!" His demeanor changed a few minutes later when he walked into a room full of reporters and fumed about the speculation.

Linebacker Jeff Davis and the Tigers used the whipping of the Gamecocks as a springboard to a national title in 1981. *Courtesy of Clemson University Sports Information Department.*

"You all know what you can do with those rumors. I don't think I have to tell you…The rumors have made this a terrible year. The bad thing about it is that it's been mostly our people who have been spreading them."

Later, as he recorded his weekly TV show reviewing the game with radio play-by-play man Jim Phillips, Ford opened the show by voicing his displeasure with the rumors and the people who perpetuated them.

Clemson's momentum from the stunning victory carried into the off-season and on into the fall of 1981, when the Tigers captivated the college football world by going 12-0 and claiming a national title.

Carlen made it one more season, his visions of sustained greatness giving way to his departure after his 1981 team finished 6-6 with three straight losses to close the season—including a 29–13 home throttling to Clemson on the Tigers' march to the pinnacle.

The orange pants became synonymous with big-time games and big-time wins as Ford built a powerhouse. He reserved them for special games only, and the Tigers' high rate of success in them fostered the belief that they bestowed mystical powers.

Gough, the equipment manger who pulled the dusty orange britches from his desk drawer in the fall of 1980, went on to a successful career in sports marketing. His first venture into the profession remains his most memorable. "We were trying to get a little spark," he said, "and that's part of what the orange pants were about."

15

A SEASON SAVED

1984

SOUTH CAROLINA WON MORE games in 1984 than any team in the program's history. Despite those school-record ten victories, it's the one regular-season loss that virtually everyone associates with it.

Even the members of that team readily admit that any mention of the 1984 season quickly shifts to a four-letter word: Navy.

The Gamecocks were 9-0 and ranked second in the country. After big wins, the team would return home to the airport greeted by thousands of fans. More lined the streets from the airport to campus.

These kids were like rock stars. Joe Morrison created some optimism in 1983 by winning five games, including a 38–14 annihilation of Southern Cal. But no one expected anything close to the story that was unfolding.

"We felt like we had something to prove every week," junior quarterback Mike Hold said. "It was just cool to be on that ride. Every Monday morning, we'd get up to see the polls in the paper, to see where we'd gone. We would be a little bit pissed after we wouldn't go as high as we thought we should."

Carolina was finally living its dream season, two victories from a perfect regular season and a berth in the Orange Bowl, to potentially play for a national championship. The two remaining opponents: Navy and Clemson.

The U.S. Naval Academy figured to be the easy part, even if the game on November 17 was in Annapolis, Maryland. The Midshipmen had won three games, and injuries had greatly handicapped the team all season. One columnist that week called Navy "a football cripple." The Gamecocks seemed to be viewing them as such in the days approaching the game. They had defeated Georgia and Florida State, both ranked in the top fifteen at the time, as well as Pitt and Notre Dame. Navy? The Gamecocks were the toast of the Palmetto State, not to mention the darling of the national media, after wiping the Seminoles off the field in a nationally televised showdown the previous Saturday.

Three years after Clemson made a completely unanticipated undefeated run to the national title, the rivals down the road in Columbia were taking their turn. The Gamecocks had Morrison, a mysterious but beloved figure who lived hard, wore all black and puffed Marlboros on the sideline during games. They had the "Fire Ants" defense that swarmed to the ball with ferocity in the all-garnet uniforms. And they had "Black Magic," a mythical and intoxicating aura that was burnished by stirring comeback victories at Notre Dame and North Carolina State.

And now, as they exulted over blowing number eleven Florida State out of Williams-Brice Stadium on perhaps the most glorious night in Gamecocks football history, they knew their ticket to Miami would be punched with a victory over Navy. The Orange Bowl wanted to match up Carolina with number one Nebraska for the national title, and not many of the questions from the media that week were about Navy. Everyone wanted to know what the Gamecocks thought of the next game, that trip up to Death Valley seven days later.

At various points during the dismantling of Florida State, fans tossed oranges onto the field—the same way Clemson fans had tossed them in 1981 when they won in Columbia on their way to Miami, where they beat Nebraska to finish number one.

So it wasn't nearly as easy for players and coaches to focus on Navy then as it has been ever since. Not even with Morrison preaching in press conferences that week that Navy might be the most dangerous team on the schedule. The Midshipmen were missing five starters because of injuries, including star tailback Napoleon McCallum.

Morrison made a big mistake, though. Two days before the game, he informed his team that they were bound for the Orange Bowl with a win over Navy.

"The night before, a couple of our seniors were joking around a little bit," said defensive back Brad Edwards, a freshman in 1984. "I remember turning to a guy next to me and saying, 'I don't think we're going to play well tomorrow. I don't think these guys are getting ready to play.' We were not. We were not ready to play."

Mike Hold was a quarterback on the 1984 Carolina team that won a school-record ten games. Hold scored the winning touchdown in a 22–21 victory against Clemson. *Courtesy of Mike Safran.*

Edwards was not exaggerating. On a frigid day near the Chesapeake Bay, Navy held a 14–7 lead at the half and opened it up to a 38–7 advantage by the fourth quarter. The Gamecocks were left flat-footed by how physical the Middies were, bull-rushing between the tackles to pick up chunks of yards. In doing so, Navy played keep-away from a Carolina option offense that came in carrying the team, averaging 447.7 yards and 34.8 points a game.

A thirty-one-point hole in the final quarter was far too much to overcome, and the Gamecocks stumbled 38–21.

To Navy. And that wasn't the worst of it. A few days before, the Sugar Bowl had approached Carolina and said it would take the Gamecocks regardless of what happened at Navy. Morrison said no thanks. He was holding out for the Orange Bowl against the Cornhuskers.

"It was a dark afternoon for black magic," the game story in *The State* said the following day. "Down the tubes went a historic all-win season." Navy recognized it had been overlooked. "I don't think they took us seriously," captain and defensive tackle Eric Rutherford said. "I think they thought they would walk on us."

The national title hopes were snuffed after the loss to Navy, but the season was not. Clemson remained. The Gamecocks, reeling, had to figure out a way to bounce back for the rivalry game. The Sugar Bowl had backed off, and Carolina's bowl destination was uncertain.

NATURALLY, CAROLINA'S PRACTICES BETWEEN the Navy and Clemson games were not exactly crisp. "I think most of us were in somewhat of a funk most of the week," senior receiver Bill Bradshaw said. "It was unlike any Clemson-Carolina week that I'd experienced. We were so distraught and disappointed for what we had allowed to happen."

In a meeting early that week, Morrison wrote some words on a chalkboard:

Orange Bowl
Number 1 Ranking
National Championship

One by one, he crossed through them and told the players they'd made a $2 million mistake. "All gone," Morrison then wrote, underlining it a couple of times. "Reality kind of slapped us in the face. We just blew something big," Hold said. "It was about as tough of a circumstance as you could find. It was a very deflated team." Hold and Bradshaw said that week, as it continued, was about processing and refocusing.

The leadership tried to prop up the team, reminding it that the school had defeated Clemson just once since Jeff Grantz and the Gamecocks ran wild in 1975. That group of seniors had never defeated the Tigers, had never really ever been close. Bradshaw's teams had lost to their rivals by sixteen, eighteen and nine points. So it meant something on that historical front. Carolina also was still pushing for a decent bowl bid, even if the Orange and Sugar opportunities had vanished that day in Maryland. "We didn't want to win nine in a row and then lose two straight to end the regular season," Hold said. "If we lost to Clemson, the season wasn't worth a hoot. It brought us back."

The Tigers started the season ranked fourth in the country and rose to number two before dropping consecutive games in the state of Georgia, to Georgia and Georgia Tech, both ranked number twenty at the time. Clemson won the next five games to get back into the polls, at number twenty, but then Maryland smoked the Tigers, 43–21, in Baltimore on the same day the Gamecocks were losing at Navy not far away.

Trying to pull his team together, Clemson coach Danny Ford did not allow his players to speak with the media the week of the Carolina game. The Gamecocks were not the only ones trying to salvage a promising season, even if Clemson was still on probation and unable to go to a bowl as penance for NCAA violations discovered after its national title. The Tigers actually entered the game as two-point favorites, despite the fact that Carolina was ranked ninth that week in the United Press International poll. Clemson's seniors had gone unbeaten in twenty-six home games over four seasons, and they had owned the Gamecocks.

It was hard for Carolina fans to be abundantly confident as they filed into Death Valley that day. Clemson's band played Navy's "Anchors Aweigh" as a reminder of the disaster that had unfolded seven days before. Orange-clad fans tossed oranges and lemons onto the field. A sign read: "Welcome to your Orange Bowl, South Carolina." And the Tigers broke out their orange pants for the occasion, pants they hadn't lost in since they wore them for the first time in a 1980 domination of the Gamecocks on the same field.

The Navy hangover was in full effect for the Gamecocks, who very quickly found themselves in a 21–3 canyon. Bradshaw said that past Carolina teams would have quit at that point, but the 1984 group proved that day it was different. It had won games that season in all sorts of weird, crazy ways. Down eighteen on the road, the Gamecocks did not count themselves out.

The pivotal moment transpired forty-two seconds before the half. Scott Hagler kicked his second field goal, making it 21–6 Tigers—but Clemson was penalized for roughing the kicker. The points came off the scoreboard, and Carolina was awarded a first down. With time running out, the Gamecocks faced fourth and four on the Clemson five. Morrison sent in the call. Carolina was going for it. Bradshaw remembers his eyes getting wide when he heard the play: a trap handoff to Quinton Lewis, designed to go right past Clemson's mountain of a nose guard, William "Refrigerator" Perry. It was the boldest possible call in such a critical time.

The play worked. Perry picked a side. Lineman Tommy Garner cleared him out of the way, opening up a lane for Lewis to get into the end zone. The score, cutting the lead to 21–10, changed everything. Tony Guyton tackled Clemson quarterback Mike Eppley for a safety early in the second half, continuing momentum's surge toward the Carolina sideline. Another Hagler field goal, from forty-one yards out, got the Gamecocks to within a score with seven minutes remaining.

Eppley, then a senior, remembers the Gamecocks' defense being much faster than usual.

"They were just like our defense—very physical, very fast," he said. "They flew to the ball quickly, a swarming defense. You had a split second to make decisions on everything."

CLEMSON COULD NOT CONVERT on a key third down and was forced to punt. South Carolina took over on the following possession at its own sixteen-yard line, eighty-four yards from tying the game and an extra point away from winning it. The drive nearly ended before it really started. Facing a third and seven, Hold hit Chris Wade on a post route for a thirty-seven-yard gain, pushing the Gamecocks into Clemson territory. From there, they began to carve up Perry and the Tigers. Lewis reeled off a sixteen-yard run. Thomas Dendy had an eighteen-yard run. "Everybody was doing what they were supposed to do," Hold said of the drive.

Hold finished it, taking an option keeper seven yards for a touchdown to tie the game at twenty-one. "I remember thinking, 'If there's space, I'm not going to take the chance of mishandling the ball. I'm getting in the end zone if there's space,'" Hold said. "It was our last shot. We were so close. I was just looking for an opening."

Bradshaw had run a route to the corner of the end zone and turned around just in time to see Hold stumble across the goal line. Because of an injury to Ira Hillary, he had played every snap of the game on a sizzling day in the Upstate. Bradshaw was spitting up blood after the game because of the heat and a shot he took to the kidneys. But all that did not prevent him from one unique celebration following Hold's touchdown.

Bradshaw did back flips through the back of Clemson's end zone.

Growing up in Spartanburg, he had heard all about Clemson's dominance in the rivalry over the years. In his last game against the Tigers, he was part of history to the contrary. It all came out in the form of those acrobatics. "I didn't even know where I was," Bradshaw said. "I was in la-la land. I was

The scoreboard at Death Valley, seconds after the game—and seconds before it would be shut off. *Courtesy of the University of South Carolina Archives, South Caroliniana Library.*

literally so elated that we had finally gotten to a point where we were going to beat Clemson. I was in my own little world. Oh, man, why in the world would anybody do that? It was just a crazy reaction."

There was still a matter of the point-after try if Carolina wanted to win the game. Hagler had made forty-two consecutive extra points, but he weakly missed that one low and left. He has always insisted that is because he heard a whistle as he was going through his kicking motion. Clemson had twelve men on the field and could not get the extra man off quickly enough. The Tigers were penalized, and Hagler got another kick. The second try sailed through the uprights, high and good. Clemson could not get into range for a field goal, and the Gamecocks got the ball back for the final seconds. Perry, who would quickly rise to NFL fame the next year with the Chicago Bears, tussled with Hold as the clock struck zero. Hold dangled the ball in front of Perry and dropped it to the brown turf as the Gamecocks began to celebrate.

Carolina had finished its miraculous comeback to win 22–21 at Clemson. It was the Gamecocks' first victory at Death Valley since 1970, capping a 10-1 regular season, the best in the program's history. They didn't get to chase a national title, but the magic returned that day. Clemson closed its year at 7-4 after amassing a 30-2-2 record the previous three seasons.

"They had things fall their way that season, kind of like we did in 1981," Eppley said. "They had a good group of seniors who were not really superstars, but a really cohesive unit. And I think probation all those years probably kind of caught up to us. Mentally, physically and spiritually, it all took its bearing on us that year."

Carolina slipped to the Gator Bowl and could not overcome a poor first half in a 21–14 loss to Thurman Thomas and Oklahoma State—a squad Morrison later said "was the best team we played all year."

But the Gamecocks needed that Clemson win to get to ten victories, to get something back. Yes, the 1984 team suffered the Navy loss that still seems incomprehensible all these years later. But it also had the Clemson comeback.

"Had we beaten Navy and lost to Clemson, I don't think the season would be talked about the way it is," Hold said. "That's how important that Clemson win is to that season. I just don't think the season would have ever been remembered the same way. It doesn't matter what you do as long as you beat Clemson."

16

BLACK DEATH...AND RODNEY'S REVENGE

1987–88

O N A SUNDAY AFTERNOON in late November 1987, Rodney Williams cranked up his parents' boat and went for a ride on Lake Murray all by himself.

The middle of a massive, man-made lake was probably the only place Williams could venture in his hometown of Columbia without hearing the numbing chant: "Raaaaahhhdnaaaay. RAAAAAAAAHHHHHHHHHdnaaaaaaaay."

The night before, in the raucous and bloodthirsty din of Williams-Brice Stadium, Williams suffered through the most helpless, humiliating experience of his football life. There was nowhere for him to hide as a stadium full of black-clad fans celebrated a mauling of Clemson by serenading the local kid with derisive and endless chants of his first name. A national television audience watched as Williams unraveled against the team he grew up hating.

"For all general purposes, they wanted to string me up," Williams remembers. "That was a tough time. It was a tough couple of weeks."

Williams's parents were in the stadium that night, and a difficult experience was made worse when a Gamecock fan poured a Coke over the head of his mother late in the game. His father, Gene Williams, vowed as they left never to step foot in the place again. It is a promise he has kept, even while running a beer distributorship that sits in the shadow of the stadium.

"Ain't enough money in the world for me to go back in there," he said. "Only way is if one of my family had a health issue and me going in there would cure it. I'd do it, but it'd have to be guaranteed."

A few hours after the game, father and son huddled in a corner during a somber postgame party in West Columbia. Rodney was in a daze, still in some shock and hurting physically and mentally from the beating he absorbed on a cold night in Columbia. "Wash it off," his father advised. "Forget about it. Go on and think about something else. And remember just one thing: We've got 364 days. Work your ass off to make sure you pay them back for it."

THE TIGERS-GAMECOCKS RIVALRY BURNED white-hot in the 1980s, when both programs achieved unprecedented and unduplicated success. Clemson rose up to claim its national title in 1981. Carolina's Black Magic came three years later with a ten-win season in which the Gamecocks vaulted to number two in the polls and came close to playing for their own title. And 1987 presented a true rarity: heavyweights on both sides of this bitter feud.

The Tigers came in ranked number eight, fresh off a dominating victory over Maryland that sealed their second consecutive ACC title. The Gamecocks were ranked twelfth but were a touchdown favorite on a blistering roll, having savaged five consecutive opponents by a combined score of 210–32. Head coach Joe Morrison, then in his fifth year, had struck gold with the off-season hiring of defensive coordinator Joe Lee Dunn and his chaotic, stunting "50" defense that was abusing opposing offenses and battering quarterbacks. The Gamecocks' only two losses were narrow road defeats at Georgia and Nebraska.

The previous Saturday, Carolina had gone to Wake Forest and ripped apart an above-average team 30–0. Demon Deacons coach Bill Dooley, that season's ACC coach of the year, was impressed. "I've said it before and I'll say it again: South Carolina is one of the best five teams in the country," he said at the time.

Clemson had owned Carolina from 1976 to 1985, winning eight times in ten meetings. And even after the Tigers were fortunate to forge a 21–21 tie in the 1986 game at Death Valley, it was Clemson that began the 1987 season facing forecasts of national title contention. The Tigers had taken their hits from the three-year NCAA and ACC probation that followed their 1981 championship, and now coach Danny Ford was loaded again in his ninth season.

The Gamecocks had stockpiled their own fleet of talented players. The offense was prolific with quarterback Todd Ellis, wingback Sterling Sharpe, running back Harold Green and receiver Ryan Bethea. The defense was fast and athletic, perfect for Dunn's oddball scheme. And the Gamecocks were hungry and bent on payback after suffering through a 3-6-2 record in 1986 that featured an extraordinary number of close and painful defeats.

Though uplifted by the convincing win over Maryland, Clemson fans were nervous as they pondered what awaited them in Columbia. The Tigers bagged a big win over Georgia in September, but they were shaky in narrow victories over average Duke and North Carolina teams and awful in falling behind 30–0 at home against NC State and losing 30–28. Ron Green Jr., who covered Clemson for the *Greenville News*, asked an unnamed Clemson official to describe the feeling inside the school's athletics department early in the week. The reply: "Fear."

Danny Ford participates in a pep rally on Clemson's campus a few days before the game against Carolina in the late 1980s. *Courtesy of Clemson University Sports Information Department.*

The apprehension seemed to extend to the coaching staff. Ford applied a media gag order on his players and assistants the entire week, leading *Charleston News and Courier* columnist Gene Sapakoff to brand Ford the "Prince of Paranoia."

"Just when you think the Clemson football program is pounding out the negative dents in its image, Danny Ford treats his players like a bunch of irresponsible children," Sapakoff wrote. "This is as embarrassing as probation."

Ford's reasoning held that the Gamecocks benefited from significant advance scouting of Clemson by having faced six common opponents after the Tigers had already played them. Not once that season had Clemson been able to take notes on the Gamecocks in similar fashion. In Ford's mind, Clemson's staff and players were behind in preparation and needed extra time to catch up. He told his coaches to forget about reviewing the Maryland film on Sunday and to get started on the Gamecocks. Ford said at the time that it was the biggest challenge he'd ever faced as a head coach—bigger than the Orange Bowl date with Nebraska at the end of the 1981 season, and bigger than a series of titanic clashes with the Georgia Bulldogs.

"I can see how they think, the people in Columbia think, and the general consensus of the state thinks they can probably name whatever they want to name against Clemson," Ford told reporters. "They have a great amount of confidence that they're going to blow us out from the talk I hear."

The Gamecocks' confidence was on full display in the papers that week. Center Woody Myers talked trash about Clemson defensive lineman Michael Dean Perry, who would earn All-America and ACC player of the year honors in 1987. He also wasn't impressed with the Tigers' whitewashing of Maryland. "They better be a little more realistic," he told reporters. "They played well against Maryland, but we're not Maryland."

RODNEY WILLIAMS WAS NEVER the type to lob barbs at his opponent through the media. As much as he despised the Gamecocks while growing up in Spartanburg, then moving to the Columbia suburbs and starring as quarterback at Irmo High School, he said the hatred began to wear off when he arrived at Clemson in 1984. Part of the reason was the development of strong bonds with players on the other side and the realization that "they were working just as hard as I was."

Williams, Ellis and Gamecocks safety Brad Edwards became friends long before they faced one another in the rivalry, having met at a passing camp in Charlotte in the early 1980s. Williams remembers spending the summers goofing off with Edwards and a number of other Gamecocks, behaving like typical college kids.

"My high school friends had kind of drifted away when I was in college, and my friends became the football team," Williams said. "So when I would go home, the people I had the most in common with were the football players at South Carolina. I would call them up and that's who I would hang out with. We'd go play pickup basketball games, go to the lake together, go to bars—that's who I would interact with. It grew into about eight or ten guys that I used to hang out with in Columbia and got to know real well."

Edwards, a North Carolina native who played quarterback in high school, remembers being a regular fixture in Williams's home as a fifteen- and sixteen-year-old. He also remembers attending fraternity and sorority parties at Clemson with Williams, and Williams doing the same with him in Columbia.

"We had a strong friendship throughout college, which is difficult when you go to the schools that we attended," Edwards said. "I slept in their dorm; they slept in our dorm. I guess you'd call that the dirty little secret in the rivalry."

Another secret: playful jabbering between combatants during otherwise tense moments on the football field. The stakes and the competitive fire never precluded a few conversations about that night's keg party.

"We used to think it was pretty cool, because half of my friends on those teams were on offense and half on defense," Williams said. "The defensive guys would try to take my head off, but there were numerous times where they're laying on me after tackling me and we'd laugh and talk about what we were doing together after the game."

Minutes before the 1986 game in Clemson, Williams and Ellis noticed each other and met at midfield. Ellis was a freshman who was breaking all kinds of passing records, Williams a sophomore who had guided the Tigers to an ACC title. They shook hands. Ellis looked around an overflowing Death Valley, took in the moment and said, "You realize we're the two most powerful people in the state of South Carolina right now, don't you?"

As the buildup began early in the week of the 1987 game, bad news struck at Clemson when Williams suffered a hyper-extended knee during Monday's practice. He was on the shelf Tuesday and Wednesday, and Ford condensed his offensive game plan as a result.

"Coach Ford was the kind of coach that if he didn't see it work successfully in practice and you didn't execute it time and time again, he wasn't going to let you call it," Williams said.

The conservative approach played right into the hands of the Gamecocks, whose defensive strategy under Dunn was to stuff the run and get to the quarterback before he could get a pass away. "I don't think Clemson wants to throw the ball against us," Dunn said at the time. "Everybody uses play-action, but nobody has done that well against us because it's hard to run play-action and block all the people we bring on the rush at the same time."

Clemson made a resounding statement on its first possession, driving ninety-one yards on eighteen plays for a touchdown. But the Tigers' offense did almost nothing from there, and Williams slowly descended into his own personal hell that was complete with a personalized soundtrack. The Gamecocks took a 13–7 lead in the third quarter to grab the momentum, and at this point the chants began to take hold. Keith Jennings, then a junior tight end who went on to play in the NFL, vividly remembers the point when everyone in the offensive huddle deciphered the chants and realized the target was their own quarterback.

"Everyone's eyes got real big," Jennings said. "We're like…daaaaammn man. They're talking about you!" Williams looked around at his teammates and smiled. "You don't think they like me, do you?"

On the other side of the ball, Edwards's heart sank a bit when he heard the black-clad, towel-waving masses going after his friend. "I sort of cringed," he said. "You don't ever want to see someone singled out personally on a football field or in athletics."

Two years earlier in Columbia, Williams had been a nineteen-year-old freshman starting for the Tigers. He was so jacked up for the return to his hometown that his legs were numb and weak as he dashed from the locker room before the game. He was nervous for the first and last time of his football career, and Ford temporarily benched his jittery quarterback early. Williams gathered his bearings on the sideline, returned and led the Tigers to a close victory.

"I had built it all up too much in my head," Williams said. "Looking around, I was finally there. What was I going to do? I was glassy-eyed and bug-eyed. I couldn't calm down. It was a great lesson for me, because a quarterback always has to be under control."

Late in the 1987 game, the chants enveloped the stadium as Williams faced third and thirteen with Clemson at its thirty. The Tigers still had a chance with less than six minutes left. That chance evaporated when Williams dropped back and threw right to Edwards, who dashed forty yards to the end zone to spark bedlam in Williams-Brice.

He never saw Edwards. "They had been blitzing all night and Brad lined up like he was going to blitz. He dropped back into a zone, which they'd showed only a few times in the first half."

After completing three passes for fifty-four yards on the first possession, Williams succeeded on just four of his final seventeen attempts, for forty-seven yards, and finished with three interceptions. Two were to his buddy Edwards.

The Gamecocks had just drubbed their rivals to conclude a smothering run against foes from the ACC. Chants of "ACC! ACC!" shook Carolina's locker room. The Gamecocks had pillaged Virginia, NC State, Wake Forest and Clemson by a total of 156–17. "We're ACC champs now," Sterling Sharpe told reporters. "You'd better believe it."

Later that night, as reporters in the Williams-Brice press box wrote of the Gamecocks finally emerging from Clemson's shadow and becoming the glamour program in the Palmetto State, a jolting sight greeted revelers at a Five Points bar: Edwards and Williams together, grabbing a beer.

Two weeks later, the number eight Gamecocks went to Miami and came up four points short against number two Miami. The Hurricanes went on to win the national title, and the Gamecocks suffered a 30–13 beating against LSU in the Gator Bowl to finish 8-4. Williams gained some redemption by leading the Tigers to a 35–10 gouging of Penn State in the Citrus Bowl, allowing Clemson to close with a ten-win season.

Edwards's eligibility was up, and he went on to a lengthy career in the NFL. Williams still had one more season in Clemson, and November 19 was circled on his calendar the moment the 1988 schedule was released.

THOUGH HE'D LED CLEMSON to an 18-2-2 record and two ACC titles as a sophomore and junior, Williams was far from beloved by Clemson fans. He was inconsistent as a passer. He wasn't sleek or spectacular. He certainly didn't put up the gaudy passing numbers Ellis was rolling up in Columbia.

And he was held responsible for the humiliation in Columbia the previous November. "The whole time I was there they booed me," Williams said.

The Tigers had aspirations of greatness as the 1988 season began with many of the key pieces back from 1987. From the beginning, Ford spiced his talks to the team with two main goals: win the ACC, and make the Gamecocks pay dearly for 1987.

"Coach Ford was always finding ways to motivate, and he didn't need much," said Vance Hammond, a sophomore defensive lineman on the 1988 team. "If you gave us a reason to get fired up, whether it be a little press release or an article or whatever, he would elevate it tenfold."

"We wanted to smack them in the mouth because the year before we had won the ACC and weren't ready for them in Columbia. Coach Ford preached all year: 'We're going to win the ACC, smack USC in the mouth and finish the season.'"

By early October, another epic Tigers-Gamecocks matchup was taking shape. Carolina began the season in the Top 20 and rose to number eight after starting 6-0 and dealing a 23–10 demolition to number six Georgia in Columbia. Clemson was also in the Top 10 after a 5-1 start, the only blemish a home loss to Florida State that was sealed on the famous "Puntrooskie" play called by Seminoles coach Bobby Bowden.

And then everything the Gamecocks built came crashing down. Seemingly out of nowhere came a 34–0 beating at Georgia Tech in the seventh game.

Danny Ford talks to quarterback Rodney Williams on the sidelines. *Courtesy of Clemson University Sports Information Department.*

Days later, *Sports Illustrated* rocked the program with a story in which former Gamecock defensive lineman Tommy Chaikin alleged rampant steroid usage on the team.

Engulfed by the brewing scandal during an open date that followed the debacle in Atlanta, the Gamecocks punched back with a defiant 23–7 romp of North Carolina State in Raleigh on ESPN. They were ranked number fifteen the next week when number five Florida State came to Columbia for a nationally televised showdown. The Seminoles silenced the capacity crowd early by going up big and ended up tattooing the Gamecocks with 59–0 score. Carolina wore all black the next week for a shaky home victory over Navy, and the attire was fitting because everyone present seemed to still be in mourning over what happened against the Seminoles.

CLEMSON HAD WRAPPED UP its third straight ACC title when it turned its attention to the Gamecocks. Carolina came to Death Valley with eight wins, and the meeting attracted big-game buildup. But the Tigers knew the Gamecocks were a mere shell of their 1987 selves. The Gamecocks seemed to know it, too.

"I just remember our focus and how we were going to take it to them," said Levon Kirkland, a freshman linebacker on the 1988 team. "There was no way in hell that these guys were going to beat us. Not only that, but they had to pay a price for the last time they played us."

The Tigers were further energized before the game when Ford informed them that his mother had suffered a heart attack in Alabama on Friday. He told the team he'd promised his mother a victory over the Gamecocks, whipping his players into a frenzy.

Carolina marched deep into Clemson territory on its first possession but squandered the opportunity on a lost fumble by Harold Green. The Tigers

Rodney Williams wears a look of satisfaction with victory over the Gamecocks sealed in 1988. *Courtesy of Clemson University Sports Information Department.*

seized control early thanks in part to pinpoint passes by Williams, who was as sharp and authoritative as he had been erratic and unsure the previous year in Columbia.

"They played the exact same defense, and we had a better plan," Williams said. "I wasn't hurt, and they had lost a couple of key guys so they weren't as strong and as talented as they were my junior year. If they were going to bring all that pressure, we were going to just throw a lot of quick passes and basically get them out of it. We pretty much had them the whole time. It wasn't that close."

THE END OF AN era was at hand for the Gamecocks. Morrison, facing the fallout from the steroid scandal and the likely loss of his job, would die in February after collapsing in a shower at Williams-Brice Stadium. The magic and the black and the glimpses of greatness were gone—and so was the success against Clemson, which went to Columbia in 1989 and dealt the Gamecocks a pulverizing 45–0 defeat that was even more decisive than the score indicated.

As he jogged off the field for the last time at Death Valley, having contributed greatly to a 29–10 spanking that turned the balance of the rivalry back in Clemson's favor, Williams was on top of the world. He smiled broadly as he took his seat on the bench and heard his first name chanted once again—this time by an adoring home crowd.

Williams turned around and looked in the direction of his family, who sat in a luxury box high above the Clemson sideline. He gave a thumbs-up that was returned by his father. "It was a dream," Gene Williams said. "I sat there and cried. It was like something you write a movie script for. Like a cowboy movie, when you shoot the bad guy and the credits roll."

17

TANEYHILL'S HOME RUN

1992

WHEN SPARKY WOODS TOOK over as South Carolina's head coach in 1989, after the unexpected death of Joe Morrison, he started keeping a notebook beside his bed.

In the evening, the morning or the middle of the night, Woods, previously at Appalachian State, would jot down something that he thought would help close the wide gap between Carolina and Clemson. It could be something as simple as a wrinkle to a play. It could be something as significant as a commitment from a coveted recruit. "I knew in that state that was the game you had to win," said Woods, from east Tennessee. "I just made a point every day to write down how we were catching up. It was a constant reminder. 'What'd you do today to try and beat Clemson?'"

Woods cannot recall exactly how Steve Taneyhill's commitment to Carolina was documented in the notebook, but rest assured that he received more than a passing mention. Alabama wanted Taneyhill from the famed, fertile quarterback territory of western Pennsylvania. Florida State wanted him, too. So did Miami. But the Gamecocks got him. The other schools seemed set at quarterback for the years to come. Carolina, to him, needed one…yesterday.

His introduction to fans? "I'm going to start here next year," he told *The State* after watching the spring game shortly after he signed. That did not exactly endear him to his new teammates and especially the other quarterbacks. But, in a breath, it was Taneyhill: sure of himself, unafraid to say so.

A full-length *Sports Illustrated* feature story by Sally Jenkins preceded Taneyhill's sophomore season, in 1993. It summed him up like this: "A prized but controversial freshman recruit with a lush mane, a bold mouth and, to complete the ensemble, a faux diamond stud in his left ear."

He was like nothing the Gamecocks had ever seen, much less had on their sideline.

"He was that next Pennsylvania quarterback to come out, and he signs with South Carolina?" said Clemson defensive tackle Brentson Buckner, Taneyhill's verbal sparring partner throughout his college career. "It was a big deal, the Yankee from up North coming into South Carolina. I hated him because he played for South Carolina, but I sort of respected him because he was a brash guy who said, 'I'm doing good things and I'm going to let you know it.' He had that confidence."

And the hair, of course. The stringy mullet emerging from the back of his helmet became his identity, which sometimes worked for and against him. Carolina fans loved it and let him know. Opposing fans hated it and let him know. Still, Woods knew better than to force him to cut the iconic blondish mane. He was wise enough to let Taneyhill be Taneyhill.

"I don't have any hair," Woods said, "so I don't make fun of anybody's hair."

IT DIDN'T TAKE TOO long for Taneyhill to make good on his spring promise, although the team almost fell apart before he made his first start. The Gamecocks, playing their first season in the talent- and history-rich Southeastern Conference, lost the first five games of the year.

After a 48–7 thumping on October 3 at Alabama, which went on to win the national title, there was near-mutiny. An off-week story in *The State* chronicled the senior class's hardships, including the 1989 death of Morrison, Woods's arrival and the brutally rough welcome to the SEC.

Looking back, Woods said he thought the story was fair and actually complimentary of the seniors. His take on what went awry: Some people inside the program wanted Woods, who had lost nine consecutive games at that point, gone. They ran a behind-the-scenes smear campaign against him, trying to get the players to turn on him the same way that teams at Arkansas and Memphis had (successfully) revolted against their coaches.

When the players returned from a weekend break due to the bye, a tension-filled heart-to-heart session was held to clear the air and attempt to bring the team back together for the second half of the season. Woods called it a "finger-pointing meeting." The edgy experience ended with Woods issuing a challenge before that evening's practice. "If you don't come, then pick your stuff up and go on," he told the players. "We'll move on with the ones left. But you'd better be here." Then he waited. And hoped.

Everyone appeared and practiced, renewed for the rest of the season. It was a different team going forward. Accompanying the theme of newness, Woods announced that Taneyhill would start that Saturday against Mississippi State. "Finally," Taneyhill thought. "I'd be over there watching, thinking, 'I'd have done this, I'd have done that,'" Taneyhill said. "I'd tell the coaches that, too. 'You need to play me. You need to play me.' I wanted that challenge. That was just the competitor in me. I'd tell you I could play today. I probably couldn't—well, I don't think I could—but I would tell you I could."

With very little left to lose, Woods and his staff relented to Taneyhill's tugging on their pant legs. They did not regret it, either.

With Taneyhill in charge, the Gamecocks got their first victory of the season. Heck, it was their first victory in 364 days, going back to the previous October. They defeated a good team, too, upsetting fifteenth-ranked Mississippi State. The second play of the game, a thirty-five-yard completion, set the tone for a 21–6 victory.

A longhaired quarterback leading the offense and a shutdown defense already in place, the Gamecocks suddenly played with Taneyhill's swagger. "He kind of got us going," Woods said. Beginning with Mississippi State, they won four consecutive games, including another upset of a ranked SEC team, number sixteen Tennessee.

Chris Rumph, a third-year sophomore linebacker for the Gamecocks who got his first career start in the 1992 game against Clemson, remembers Taneyhill galvanizing the team on and off the field:

> *Steve came in at the right moment. He was exactly what we needed. Our backs were against the wall—so what? We were going to scratch and fight and claw and do whatever we had to do. We loved it on defense because we felt Steve's mentality was of a defensive guy playing offense. He wasn't the typical quarterback, because usually you don't see quarterbacks hanging out with different guys. Steve got right in there with us. We partied together and did all sorts of things together. You can't imagine some of the things we did.*

Even South Carolina's losses were impressive. It went to the Swamp and had a legitimate chance to surprise Steve Spurrier and eleventh-ranked Florida, before settling for a 14–9 loss.

Long-haired and outspoken, Steve Taneyhill helped the 1992 team rally to win five of its final six games, including Clemson. *Courtesy of Mike Safran.*

Clemson was paying attention. For the first time in a long time, it was not sure if it had the better team. The compilation of items in Woods's notebook had worked to level things out in the rivalry, for the time being. That thought would have seemed laughable even in early October, with an 0-5 team, but South Carolina was looking and playing differently. Clemson noticed. Three years earlier in the series, it had blasted the Gamecocks 45–0 in a game that felt as if it were 450–0. Woods, in his first year at Carolina, remembered telling the team's nose guard to lie down on the ground because he was being blocked past the safeties.

Things had changed, and they had changed fast. "That was a real big deal," said Buckner, who went on to a standout NFL career. "You looked around and said, 'Wow, we just don't have the pieces.' And we didn't."

South Carolina's fans were starting to really embrace Taneyhill's brash demeanor. They would wear hats to games with fake ponytails hanging out the back. And then a faction took it too far.

In the days leading up to that 1992 game at Death Valley, a few rogue Gamecocks fans broke into the stadium and attempted to steal Howard's Rock atop the Hill. They were not successful, but they left the exterior of the rock damaged.

The Tigers were 5-5. They had lost three of the past four games. And the vandalizing of the Rock felt like another defeat. Some team officials were in tears as they learned about it. It was part of the team, to some. (The Rock is now encased, protected.) "You felt disrespected," Buckner said. "It's a big rivalry, and I'm pretty sure all those things happen all around. But the anger and the different emotions, you felt. We wanted to hurt somebody."

Unfortunately for Clemson, it did not have the team to inflict pain and get retribution. Instead, it had front-row seats for Taneyhill Theater on that rainy November day. He had celebrated throughout those four victories after he took over, but he saved his best demonstrations for his first game against Tigers, a 24–13 Carolina victory.

Brandon Bennett and Rob DeBoer were big, burly runners for Carolina. The defense, which allowed two touchdowns a game the final six games, was again outstanding. But Taneyhill, who finished the day nineteen for twenty-nine for 296 yards and two touchdowns, was the main event.

Clemson fans booed lustily as he faked like he was hitting a home run. And when he ran over and directed the Carolina band. And when he acted like he was autographing the Tiger paw at midfield. "I was playing against South Carolina's defense, but in the back of my mind I was playing against Steve Taneyhill," said Patrick Sapp, who started at quarterback for the Tigers in that game, though he was later moved to linebacker. "I hated that guy. I hated the way he looked. I hated the mullet. I hated the way that he celebrated."

Taneyhill and the Gamecocks had the first and last laughs, and a lot in between.

"That's just having fun," he said. "That's sitting on the bench for five lousy games, getting your chance and playing well enough for a 5-1 finish. It was our bowl game. That was it. We were done. It was just having fun and enjoying the moment. I haven't seen that game in a long time, but when I do, I think, 'Boy, we were having some fun.'"

The proud Clemson seniors had never lost to South Carolina. That was a new feeling, a slap across the face. Junior receiver Terry Smith had tears in his eyes after the loss. He was projected as a second-round NFL pick but decided to return to Clemson for his senior season based on the pain of that moment. (The Tigers won 16–13 in 1993, getting revenge against Taneyhill and Carolina.)

"We'd lost some games that year, but this was the first game I saw people crying after a loss," Sapp said. "That's when it hit me how big this rivalry was and how important it was to everybody. And from that point on, I hated South Carolina. The guys hated them. The seniors and the leaders of that team felt like they let everybody down."

Taneyhill went 2-2 against Clemson in his career, strangely enough winning both trips to Death Valley. He willingly admits he was a "toe-the-line guy." Woods said—and Taneyhill independently did, too—that he would often receive phone calls from people letting him know what his quarterback was getting into, out on the town. Some of it was not true, but some of it was. Taneyhill, who has won multiple state titles as a high school coach in South Carolina, says he understands his kids more because he was and always will be one when it comes to football. "You work way too hard not to have some fun," he said. "I wouldn't change a thing."

Neither would Woods, who got plenty of fodder for his notebook.

18

TAKING THE RIDE

1999

THE WHOLE THING TOOK less than a minute. It has required a lot longer, however, for Brad Scott to live down the Ride.

As the clock ran out in Clemson's 31–21 victory against South Carolina in 1999—an already-hard-to-stomach 0-11 season for the Gamecocks—a couple of Tigers ran toward midfield in search of first-year coach Tommy Bowden. Their plan: lift Bowden and place him on their shoulders to celebrate his first victory against the rival Gamecocks. The Tigers had also attained bowl eligibility after their first and only non-conference victory of the season.

It's something of a football tradition, players wanting to show their coach gratitude by elevating him like royalty. But the gesture rarely happens on an opposing team's home field. On the archrival's turf? Forget about it.

When the players found Bowden, he shooed them away and shied from the attention. In the moment, he came up with what he thought was a better idea and certainly a more poetic plan. He pointed about thirty yards away to Scott, Clemson's tight ends coach. "It was really kind of weird," said Jason LeMay, a redshirt freshman tight end on the 1999 team. "Bowden walked away from us, pointing at Coach Scott and saying, 'Get him! Get him!'"

So they got him. And that was when things became complicated, given Scott's previous job title. LeMay and a teammate, Pat Cyrgalis, ran to Scott, vaulted him on their shoulders and marched him out toward the hash marks at Williams-Brice Stadium. Scott, though, did not ride high like

Clemson assistant Brad Scott, less than a year removed from a head-coaching tenure at South Carolina, gets a ride from players after the Tigers' 31–21 victory at Williams-Brice Stadium in 1999. *Courtesy of Clemson University Sports Information Department.*

most coaches would in that proud moment. Instead, LeMay remembers Scott slouching and sliding off their shoulder pads. He appreciated the sentiment, but he did not want the Gamecocks and their fans thinking he was rubbing in anything. The players, though, admit they were OK with that notion.

"I don't know if he wanted to do it, but we kind of wanted to," LeMay said. "We wanted to say, 'This is the coach you let go. He came back and got you.'"

THE PREVIOUS YEAR, SCOTT was on the other sideline. He was the Gamecocks' coach, and it was not a pleasant experience. The team won one game, the opener against Ball State. It dropped the final ten, including Clemson's 28–19 victory in the Upstate.

Scott went 23-32-1 in five seasons at Carolina, but he could not survive 1-10. Even the program's first-ever bowl win, in 1994, could not save him by the end of 1998. "I thought we had five good years. We just didn't win that fifth year," Scott said in 2011, having moved into an administrative role at

Clemson. "We were doing fine. You just have that one bad year, and I don't care who you are."

That "bad" year resulted in Scott turning in his garnet. Bowden, who had just come to Clemson from Tulane, was there soon after with a shade of orange and a job offer. Bowden and Scott had gotten to know each other while on "Diddy" Bobby Bowden's staff at Florida State in the early 1980s. The timing was just right, with Scott unemployed and Tommy Bowden coming to the state to take his first major head coaching post.

"It was an opportunity for me to get another job," Scott said. "I had two boys in high school and was a pretty young guy, still. If it had been any other school in the South, I think everyone [at Carolina] would have been okay with it. I think they would have been happy with their old coach, that he was still employed."

But it was Clemson. That changed everything.

An assortment of coaches, over time, have been at both Carolina and Clemson, but very few have gone straight from one to the other. Certainly, Scott is the only man to go from head coach at one to assistant at the other. "I don't know anybody that could do that," said Rick Stockstill, the head coach at Middle Tennessee State. "That's a little bit different there, a little bit of a harder transition. At first the Clemson people, they weren't truly ready to accept him. The South Carolina people dang-sure were upset with him and couldn't understand it."

Stockstill was a Clemson assistant from 1989 to 2002 and a Gamecocks assistant from 2004 to 2005. He has seen the game from both sidelines, just like a dozen or so other coaches and administrators who have received paychecks from both schools. It can take a toll, developing relationships on both sides of a bitter rivalry.

Carolina defensive coordinator Ellis Johnson wasn't smiling much after his Gamecocks went to Clemson and dominated the Tigers in 2010. The Winnsboro native has mixed feelings not just because he served as a Clemson assistant in the mid-1990s, but also because he's close friends with a number of people on the Tigers' staff—including head coach Dabo Swinney, who played and coached at Alabama when Johnson was a Crimson Tide assistant. They won the 1992 national title there when Swinney was a senior receiver and Johnson a linebackers coach.

"That game, that's a pretty tough week for me," Johnson said. "There's a lot of people on both sides of the fence that I've worked with and think a lot of. It's tough. I wind up just being glad it's over. I'm damn happy when we beat them, but I don't take joy and don't jump around. It's pretty damn serious to a lot of people. When it's over, I want to go home."

Scott laughed at the fact that he came into the state to coach at one school and now he's been at the other, the rival, three times as long. "Don't tell me the Good Lord doesn't have a sense of humor," he said. "It was a no-brainer that I would accept that job. I knew there'd be plenty of controversy about it. But when you're let go, you're kind of out there on the street by yourself. You have to do what's best for you and your family."

Doing what is best is not always easy, of course. Scott's wife and two sons stayed behind in Columbia while he coached in Clemson. Scott lived in a hotel and often commuted back and forth, up and down Interstate 26. Generally, Scott said Gamecocks fans were not too harsh when he was back in Columbia. That is, until his first game back in 1999.

The ride from the team hotel to Williams-Brice is one that Scott vividly recalls. Clemson's buses headed up Bluff Road, toward the stadium, and Scott remembers looking down to see people making all sorts of crude gestures. "You think, 'This is kind of different,'" Scott said.

Once he arrived at the venue with the Tigers, he said it became solely about business. He improbably ended the day on his players' shoulders. In those purely raw emotions after the victory, Bowden felt as if he were recognizing an assistant who had gone through a raw deal in the recent past. But in sending Cyrgalis and LeMay to Scott, it dumped salt into the wound of a winless season. The fact that Scott's Tigers were going to a bowl was thrown in the faces of the Carolina faithful, it seemed. If that were the case, Clemson was not exactly torn up about it.

"They're never happy. I might be biased, but they're never happy," LeMay said. "South Carolina, with all due respect to them, they were really, really bad."

WHEN SCOTT LEFT THEM and Lou Holtz picked them up, yes, the Gamecocks were bad. A single win in two seasons makes that point less than debatable. Scott got off to a heck of a start at Carolina, though. There were good times after he was hired from a national championship–winning staff at Florida State. Fans in the Midlands thought for sure that they had found an up-and-comer who could alter the course of their program.

After all, how could they not feel good about going to Clemson and hanging a 33–7 drubbing on the Tigers in his first season, 1994, to become bowl eligible? The Gamecocks won that postseason game, too, taking out West Virginia by a Reed Morton field goal in the CARQUEST Bowl on January 2, 1995. Fans did not care who sponsored the game; it was a bowl win, the first in a century of playing football at Carolina. It would not have happened without that Clemson win.

Florida State had played Clemson a couple of times after joining the ACC in 1992, but Scott, a native of Arcadia, Florida, still had to be educated about what the Carolina-Clemson rivalry meant heading into his first encounter with the Tigers. Then there was the fact that the Gamecocks were sitting on five wins. They were 5-5. "We had to win," Scott said. "We put a lot into the preparation that week."

On that 1994 Gamecocks team was Chris Rumph, a senior defensive lineman who would go on to accept an assistant coaching position at Clemson in 2006. Rumph said Scott helped ease his concerns and insecurities during the process of starting out at a place he spent years despising.

The worst thing Rumph heard upon joining the Tigers? "That I was disloyal and a traitor."

"I had finished at South Carolina in 1994, so there was a little bit of a gap," Rumph said.

> *But to some people, that didn't matter. There were fans on both sides who were happy. There were fans on both sides who were upset. There were happy buddies and upset buddies—both ends of the spectrum. It was tough at first. But what made it easier in the transition was Coach Scott already being there and already having done that. He was able to navigate me through some of the road bumps that I would face.*

Scott took the Gamecocks to Death Valley on the day before the 1994 game to survey the stadium. He made sure to tell his team to stay away from the Hill, so as to avoid any sort of confrontation with the Tigers. More than that, it was a *Hoosiers* moment. Clemson's playing surface had the same dimensions as every other field in the country, and Scott wanted to make sure his team was aware.

One more wrinkle: Back in August, during preseason camp, Carolina had put in a trick play that it thought it might use during the season. The eleventh game arrived, and the Gamecocks still had not employed it. Clemson would be the perfect time for the throwback on the kickoff.

With the score tied 7–7 at the half and the Gamecocks set to receive the second-half kick, Scott made the decision to use it as he headed toward the locker room. Drawing from a speech Bobby Bowden once gave before unveiling a trick play, Scott very enthusiastically informed the team. He recalls his assistants sort of rolling their eyes when he laid out the plan:

Clemson's Rod Gardner hauls in a fourth-down heave from Woody Dantzler to seal a 31–21 victory in Columbia in 1999. *Courtesy of Clemson University Sports Information Department.*

Running back Brandon Bennett would field the kick. He'd run a few steps, stop and then fire the ball across the field to Reggie Richardson. Richardson, a quick cornerback, would do the rest. The gimmick typically had a low percentage of success—it was tough to pull off, a return man throwing the ball a long distance—but the Gamecocks would give it a shot.

The play worked. It changed the game completely, too.

Bennett caught the ball and threw it to Richardson, and Richardson made it to the Clemson five-yard line. A touchdown came soon after, and the Gamecocks scored the final twenty-six points of the game for a 33–7 victory. That second half is considered one of Clemson's lowest points at home in the rivalry. The Tigers' feelings about Scott sure changed, though. He became their punching bag. They won three of the next four meetings until he was fired.

Then he took the Ride the following year, joining Clemson to make it four of five against the Gamecocks.

"A lot of people felt like I should not have done it," he said of perching on the players' shoulders.

I'm certainly not the kind of guy to do that. I've been in this state eighteen years. I've never been a controversial person, making statements about the other school. I wouldn't have done anything to embarrass that fan base. Some people don't want to speak about it. I had zero control over that. I didn't want to try to rub it in. I tried to get down as fast as I got up.

Tommy said, "Well, if there were any ties left, that cut them." I said, "Well, gee thanks."

19

CALM BEFORE THE STORM

2000

FIFTY-NINE TICKS WERE LEFT on the clock, and everyone inside Death Valley was silent save for a few thousand Gamecocks fans who were cheering and hugging and laughing and praising their good fortune.

A few moments earlier, Clemson linebacker Keith Adams had belted Carolina tailback Derek Watson at the two-yard line as Watson tried to hurtle into the end zone for a touchdown. The ball popped loose and skittered past the goal line. Somehow, tight end Thomas Hill managed to squeeze through a cluster of Clemson players to recover the ball for a touchdown that put the Gamecocks up 14–13.

All the promise and excitement Clemson's season had held just weeks earlier was gone, like air out of a balloon. And so was the noise inside a stadium that had rocked for most of a cold, overcast afternoon.

The silence was painful to a defense that had just produced a big play at the most crucial moment, only to see it wash away with the fumble recovery. It was painful to fans who'd watched their team advance into late October with an unblemished record, only to suffer a last-second home loss to Georgia Tech and a road stomping at Florida State in the previous two games. It was painful to players who were going to have to live an entire off-season knowing they lost to the reviled Gamecocks.

But to one player—and perhaps the only orange-clad person in the entire stadium—the silence and the event that produced it were not much of a bother. There was still time left on the clock, and a junior quarterback named Woody Dantzler found himself confronted with an odd, almost otherworldly blend of comfort, clarity and confidence.

"Just the quietness is what I remember," Dantzler said. "When they scored, that's when I had an overwhelming calmness. It's almost like you're sitting on a nice boat or an ocean or a lake somewhere, and you're just relaxing. Nice and calm, not too much going on. Everything is moving slow, and it's just nice and calm and relaxing."

Woody Dantzler made game-turning plays in the fourth quarter of wins over the Gamecocks in 1999 and 2000. *Courtesy of Clemson University Sports Information Department.*

THE 2000 GAME BETWEEN these two proud programs looked to be the start of something special in the rivalry. Carolina's Lou Holtz and Clemson's Tommy Bowden were in their second seasons and were turning around both programs in a hurry. Bowden engineered a 6-6 record and a second-place ACC finish in 1999, and then in 2000 he guided the Tigers to an 8-0 start and their first Top 5 ranking since the Danny Ford days.

Holtz, whom athletics director Mike McGee lured from a gig as a sports commentator, was doing in Columbia exactly what he'd done at previous stops in his legendary coaching career: breathing life into a slumbering program and making it a monster in short order. The 1999 team finished winless, extending the Gamecocks' losing streak to twenty-one games entering the 2000 season. But Holtz summoned Carolina from the ashes and became the story of college football by overseeing a 7-1 start that earned a number seventeen ranking.

The two coaches took different routes to early success. Bowden had a familiar last name that was also a hot name after he went undefeated at Tulane in 1998, and he brought to Clemson a newfangled up-tempo offense directed by a bright, quirky coordinator named Rich Rodriguez. The spread, zone-read approach resembled the old single wing, and it ultimately became commonplace across college football. But at this time, it was a funky, oddball innovation that was dismissed as a gimmick by many.

Holtz's offensive approach was more conventional, using efficient passing by junior quarterback Phil Petty, dependable receiving by veterans Jermale Kelly and Brian Scott and a bruising running game spearheaded by Watson,

Ryan Brewer and Andrew Pinnock. The Gamecocks' defense, run by Charlie Strong, made life difficult for opposing quarterbacks with a 3-3-5 alignment that sent blitzes from unpredictable places.

The Gamecocks made an early statement in the second game by knocking off number nine Georgia 21–10. After totaling six wins over the 1997, 1998 and 1999 seasons, they surpassed that total by their eighth game in 2000. None of the victims of Clemson's 8-0 start were ranked, but the Tigers faithful believed their program was finally back to prominence after eight seasons of mediocrity.

"When Tommy Bowden first came in my sophomore year in 1999, it was an exciting time," said linebacker Chad Carson. "There was a lot of momentum and change, and we were kind of put back on the national scene. And then 2000 was the year we had a lot of the players back, and it seemed like we were going up, kind of a program ascending. And Lou Holtz, that same year had them going in the same direction. There was kind of a sense that both programs were getting better."

BOTH TEAMS STUMBLED INTO the annual Palmetto State clash.

A major showdown was shaping up between Clemson and Florida State in Tallahassee on November 4. Bobby Bowden had been lucky to leave Clemson with a victory a year earlier in a 17–14 win over his son's team, and both teams were undefeated in late October. But seven days before the Tigers' trip to Florida, Georgia Tech ventured to Death Valley and won on a touchdown pass with seven seconds remaining.

Dantzler, the spectacularly talented quarterback from Orangeburg, had suffered an ankle injury a week earlier in a game at North Carolina with Clemson down 17–0. Redshirt freshman Willie Simmons replaced him in that game and engineered a dramatic comeback and a 38–24 triumph.

Dantzler missed the entire second half against Georgia Tech. He didn't make it through three quarters of a 54–7 annihilation at Florida State the next week as Bobby Bowden poured it on his son's team by leaving his starters in well into the fourth quarter. The humiliation in Tallahassee strengthened the notion that Clemson was a paper Tiger that had fattened up on weak opposition.

The Gamecocks could not close the deal at home against hated Tennessee, suffering a 17–14 loss. They went to Florida a week later with the SEC's Eastern Division on the line and were up 21–0 before collapsing and losing 41–21.

Dantzler finds room to run in the first half of the 2000 game in Clemson. *Courtesy of Clemson University Sports Information Department.*

A year before, in round one of the Bowden-Holtz chapter, Clemson needed a win in Columbia to secure a bowl trip, and Carolina needed a win to avoid a winless season. The Gamecocks pulled within 24–21 late and forced the Tigers into a fourth and ten, but Dantzler connected with Rod Gardner on a twenty-nine-yard touchdown heave that secured a 31–21 victory, giving Clemson three consecutive wins in the rivalry.

Gardner was a big, strong wide out from Jacksonville, Florida, who carried himself with an air of confidence. Before the fourth-and-ten play in 1999, Bowden called a timeout to ponder his options. Gardner spoke up by saying he wanted the ball. Bowden was hesitant, remembering a dropped pass and an offensive pass interference penalty on Gardner earlier in the game. Bowden gave in, and Gardner made the play that distinguished him as a Gamecock killer going into the 2000 game.

IN THE TEAM HOTEL the night before, freshman kicker Aaron Hunt stood before his teammates and apologized for missing two field goals in the three-point loss to Georgia Tech thirteen nights earlier. The misses, a thirty-nine-yarder with 5:21 left in the third quarter and a twenty-nine-yarder with 9:54 in the game, made a difficult season even worse for Hunt. Through ten games, his longest successful attempt was thirty yards. And he had five misses from thirty-nine yards and in.

Despite the disappointment both teams carried into the 3:30 p.m. game, it was still an extraordinary matchup in the history of this rivalry. Clemson entered ranked sixteenth and Carolina, twenty-fifth. The only previous meetings in which both teams had entered nationally ranked were 1988, 1987 and 1979.

The contest began with Carolina driving into Clemson territory but coming up empty after Jason Corse missed a field goal from forty yards. The Tigers took possession and converted four third downs on a sixteen-play, seventy-seven-yard drive that ended with running back Travis Zachery in the end zone. The Gamecocks responded when Watson, who was a celebrated high school running back in nearby Williamston, bounced outside and dashed sixty-one yards for a touchdown.

The 7–7 score stood until late in the first half, when Clemson had the ball at Carolina's forty-four. The Tigers had taken over at their own nine, but Dantzler made a big pass to Kevin Youngblood for a pickup of twenty-seven. On second and five from the forty-four, Dantzler took a three-step drop from the shotgun, looked deep down the left sideline and fired. Gardner and cornerback Sheldon Brown bumped and shoved before Gardner rose

Clemson linebacker Chad Carson forces Derek Watson out of bounds. *Courtesy of Clemson University Sports Information Department.*

to make a one-handed catch at the four-yard line. Two Dantzler throws to Gardner in the end zone fell incomplete, and Hunt came on to kick a twenty-two-yard field goal that put Clemson up 10–7 at halftime.

The Gamecocks could not capitalize on numerous opportunities to take control in the third quarter. Their defense was making stops and keeping Clemson's potent offense on the sideline. But the normally dependable Petty, who'd totaled six interceptions through the first ten games, threw three in the third quarter to waste good field position, and the Gamecocks also lost a fumble on a punt return. The Tigers finally began to move the ball again late in the quarter, and Hunt connected from thirty-one yards to make it a 13–7 game.

Carolina followed by marching from its twenty-two to Clemson's three. The Tigers were enraged by a pass-interference penalty on third and twelve from Clemson's thirty-one. It gave the Gamecocks a first down at the sixteen.

The Tigers' defense held, stuffing Pinnock on first and second down. Petty threw incomplete for Brian Scott on third down, and Holtz elected to go for the touchdown on fourth and goal from the five instead of opting for a field goal that would have pulled the Gamecocks within three. Petty threw for Kelly, and the ball fell incomplete. A flag was thrown, but it was on Kelly, and the Tigers declined it.

Clemson could not produce a first down and punted from deep in its territory. Carolina was on the move again, Petty connecting with Scott for fourteen yards and then Kelly for twenty-four. Watson went through the right side for an eight-yard pickup to the Clemson eight, and then came an interference call on Clemson that put the Gamecocks two yards from the end zone.

The Tigers' sideline howled. "They called interference on Darrel Crutchfield, and it wasn't even close to being pass interference," Dantzler said. "If that call wasn't made, they don't even score."

The next play is still in slow motion as Carson recalls it. The Tigers' defense couldn't hold Georgia Tech two weeks earlier and couldn't put up the slightest resistance against powerful Florida State one week earlier, but it came up with a huge stop on the Gamecocks' previous possession. And then, for the briefest instant after Adams jarred the ball from Watson's grasp and the ball fell to the moist turf, Carson believed Clemson's defense had found redemption:

We'd played a pretty good defensive game, and here we go. It's on our shoulders to win the game. Let's just go ahead and do it and get your name

back a little bit as a defense. And then they drove down the field, but if
we hold them and they don't score a touchdown we win the game. Keith
forces that fumble, hits the guy so hard, and that's what you're looking
for—a defining play. But then…bam, bam, bam. The ball just kind of
rolled. Four Clemson guys around it and one Carolina guy, and the ball
goes to the Carolina guy. I basically chalked it up and said, "That stinks.
We lost the game."

Rick Stockstill, a longtime Clemson assistant who was in his seventh year as receivers coach, remembers the exhilaration of seeing the ball pop free, then the utter gut punch of seeing it recovered by the Gamecocks. But there were still fifty-nine seconds on the clock. Clemson still had Dantzler and Gardner. Stockstill quickly calmed himself down and walked over to defensive coordinator Reggie Herring.

"I told him, 'Don't worry about it. Tell your boys to get a drink of water and stand here and watch, because we're going to come back and win it,'" Stockstill sad. "He didn't say a lot of good things to me."

DANTZLER SAID HE NEVER became wrapped up in the rivalry because he had friends on the other side, and maybe that contributed to the remarkable calm that descended on him in the silence that followed Carolina's touchdown. Or maybe Dantzler was one of those rare superstars who somehow managed serenity when the situation was at its bleakest.

Dantzler still isn't sure what to make of it. "There was all kinds of stuff going on around me, but it was just like I was in the middle of a hurricane with nothing going on."

After Brian Mance returned the kickoff from the four to the thirty-two, Dantzler paused before he jogged onto the field with the offense. "I remember whispering to myself: 'We're not going to lose.' I remember making eye contact with my center, Kyle Young. He looked at me, and I guess he saw the look in my eye, and he just nodded. Zachery came up to me and said, 'I'm with you.'"

Dantzler rushed for twelve yards to the forty-four on first down. But he threw incomplete to Gardner on first down and then was sacked by Cecil Caldwell as he tried to get out of bounds to stop the clock—under twenty seconds and counting.

Up in the radio booth, frustration and resignation was in the voice of play-by-play man Jim Phillips. Dantzler was unfazed. "I was surveying my

Rod Gardner comes down with a deep ball after separating from Gamecocks cornerback Andre Goodman. Aaron Hunt kicked a field goal soon thereafter to give the Tigers a breathtaking 16–14 triumph. *Courtesy of Clemson University Sports Information Department.*

options. I was looking at the clock. No timeouts meant I had to spike the ball if we completed a pass. Total focus. I guess I was just zoned into the game and was thinking as a field general."

On third and twelve from their forty-two, the Tigers came out in a four-wide set. The Gamecocks were playing a soft zone coverage designed to prevent the big play. Gardner lined up on the right side, covered by Andre Goodman. The Tigers wanted Gardner in a one-on-one matchup, so the play called for Dantzler to immediately roll left in hopes the deep safety would drift over.

Dantzler recalled, "I had my eyes on the safety the whole time. He followed me on the rollout. When I saw him get far enough over, I let the ball go because I knew one-on-one nobody was going to stop Rod—especially in that moment."

Stockstill said, "Rod really ran a good route. He got in a little stutter early and froze Goodman a little bit, giving Rod an opportunity to get even with him. And if Rod gets even with you or behind you, you've got no chance to stop him."

What happened next incited a controversy that continues to this day and will continue forever. Gardner gained separation from Goodman by extending his left arm. The ball sailed over Goodman's head, and Gardner cradled it while falling down at the eight-yard line as the safety help arrived too late.

The following was the radio interplay among Phillips, color analyst Mike Eppley and sideline reporter Rodney Williams:

> *Eppley: I thought Gardner got away with a little push-off there toward the end.*
> *Phillips: Oh yeah.*
> *Williams: I agree with you, Epp.*
> *Eppley: But we'll take it.*
> *Williams: Big-time players make big-time plays in big games. I can't say it enough…Oh, my. I'm shaking down here, guys. I'm telling you the truth.*

DANTZLER HURRIED TO THE line and spiked the ball to stop the clock. On the sideline, Clemson's freshman kicker was summoned for a twenty-five-yard attempt from the right hash. Seven seconds were on the clock, and here came the kid who'd botched the two big kicks against Georgia Tech.

Hunt had apologized the night before in the team hotel and said it would never happen again, but…

"You never know with kickers," Carson said. "Guys who have great legs and all that stuff, they might not have ice in their veins like they need to when the game is on the line. None of us had any idea. No clue."

Initially, Hunt was nervous. But Clemson had to burn its last timeout to avoid a delay-of-game penalty, and Hunt said the extra time helped him calm down and go through his mental routine. The snap was good and so was the hold. Hunt kept his head down and sent the ball up and through the uprights, sparking an explosion of joy.

The Gamecocks were enraged. Before his postgame press conference, Holtz informed school president John Palms and athletics director Mike McGee that he was going to blast the no-call on Gardner's catch.

"All the news media and the officials should have to go into the losing locker room after a heartbreaking loss and see the pain in the players," Holtz said a day later. "Seeing a young man who maybe felt he lost the game crying his eyes out, your heart goes out to him."

Goodman, who went on to a lengthy NFL career, later said he should have been in better position. But he was disconsolate in the immediate aftermath as he spoke with reporters under the west stands. "I looked at the ref, and I just knew he was going to pull the flag out. I said, 'You had to see that. You had to see that.' And he just looked at me and kind of smiled and shook his head."

Gardner said after the game that he was surprised he was able to get behind Goodman. "It's not like I haven't done it to them before. They knew who the ball was going to."

Dantzler has no problem acknowledging that Gardner pushed off. "I know he did. I saw it when I threw the ball to him. There were missed calls all over the field that day. You give and you take."

Dantzler does not remember Hunt's field goal because he didn't see it. Before the ball was even snapped, he was walking toward the locker room.

Something told him everything was going to be just fine.

"I just heard the screams," he said.

20

A BLACK EYE

2003–04

A T 6:00 A.M. ON November 20, 2004, a group of about ninety South Carolina Highway Patrolmen from across the state convened for breakfast and a briefing at Schilletter Dining Hall on Clemson's campus.

A little more than six hours later, Clemson and Carolina would kick off at Death Valley in front of more than eighty thousand fans. The responsibility of the patrolmen was to get all those people into and out of Clemson as smoothly as possible, and that was the point of the early gathering led by Lieutenant Neal Brown.

He began working Clemson games for the highway patrol in 1969. He'd seen and heard just about everything and was an expert at navigating through difficult situations. Yet Brown was a bit apprehensive on this morning. The night before, a nasty fight had broken out in an NBA game between the Indiana Pacers and the Detroit Pistons. Brown mentioned it and told his fleet of patrolmen to have their guards up more than usual, yet there was more fueling Brown's nervousness than the NBA brawl. Earlier that week, he'd sent a request to headquarters in Columbia asking for ten to fifteen extra patrolmen to be assigned to the sidelines during the game. The request was denied.

"There was something about their records," Brown recalled. "Carolina could have knocked Clemson out of a bowl. You could just sense it was going to be a volatile situation. I just had a feeling the rivalry was going to be a little more intense than usual that day."

A State of Disunion

To PROPERLY UNDERSTAND THIS dark day in the rivalry's history and everything that contributed to it, one must rewind to a year earlier when Clemson went to Columbia and dealt the Gamecocks a 63–17 shellacking that inflicted wide-ranging repercussions on Carolina's program.

The Tigers, trying to help coach Tommy Bowden save his job, entered the 2003 game on a roll that included a completely unanticipated 26–10 rout of number three Florida State. The Gamecocks were reeling, having lost four of their previous five games, and needed a win to be eligible for a bowl. A loss would cement their second straight losing season and further underscore the descent from glory achieved by Lou Holtz in 2000 and 2001, when Carolina won seventeen games and back-to-back Outback bowls over Ohio State.

Watching film of the Gamecocks' narrow home loss to Florida the previous week in 2003, Clemson's offensive brain trust noticed that Carolina changed its defensive approach by shifting its two safeties toward the sideline after the ball was snapped to provide help to the cornerbacks. The middle linebacker was not covering the deep middle vacated by the safeties, creating a large swath of opportunity for sophomore quarterback Charlie Whitehurst and his fleet of fast, athletic receivers.

To the Tigers' delight, the Gamecocks opened the game in the same coverage. And Whitehurst said he was almost embarrassed by the ease with which he helped stake the Tigers to a 21–0 first-quarter advantage by firing deep balls right down the middle for touchdowns to Derrick Hamilton (thirty-six yards), Airese Currie (twenty-eight yards) and Ben Hall (thirty-nine yards).

"Those were three different plays that we hit, all designed for the same coverage," Whitehurst said.

> We weren't expecting to hit them all, I don't think. The second touchdown, I just basically punted the ball up in the air. It was so wide open, I just flipped it up in the air and let Airese run under it. He actually looked down when the ball was in the air to see if he was going to get hit, and there was just nobody there. It's like, "Where the hell is everybody?" I turned to the sidelines and threw my hands to the side, kind of like, "What the heck are they thinking?" I'm surprised Lou or whoever didn't say, "No more of that crap. We're not playing that defense anymore." And then they did it again.

Said Currie, "We were expecting some kind of zone coverage because we had too much speed for them to man up on us. But the Cover-2 they gave us was like Christmas."

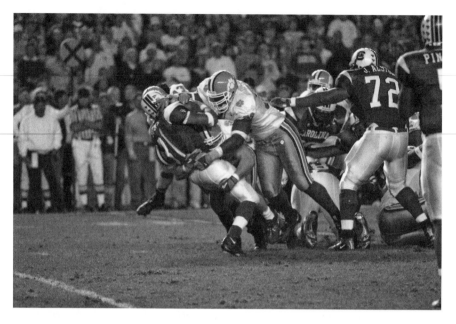

Clemson's defense set an early tone in the 2003 game by smothering Demetris Summers. *Courtesy of Clemson University Sports Information Department.*

An epic rout was on, and Carolina fans began heading home at halftime. After a Tigers touchdown early in the third quarter, the garnet and black exodus intensified and quickly left Clemson's pockets of fans to celebrate all by themselves as long ribbons of brake lights snaked away from the stadium.

Bowden, who was considered as good as gone just weeks earlier after a 45–17 meltdown at Wake Forest, left Clemson's administration no choice but to give him a contract extension. The Tigers went on to flatten number six Tennessee in the Chick-fil-A Bowl, while the Gamecocks tried to use the darkest day in their history as a rallying cry. Holtz fired three assistant coaches and reassigned another. He stripped offensive-coordinator duties from the title of his son, Skip Holtz, without informing him of it.

The 2003 dismemberment didn't just give Clemson back-to-back victories in the rivalry; it also made an unequivocal statement that the balance of power in the Palmetto State was firmly back in the Tigers' favor. Clemson derived great glee from denying the Gamecocks a bowl trip for the second year in a row. And Bowden, whose hiring at Clemson after the 1998 season was overshadowed by the spectacle of Holtz's arrival in Columbia, had the personal satisfaction of knowing he was 4-1 against the coaching legend. He was also responsible for handing Holtz the highest margin of defeat (forty-six points) and points allowed in his career.

"This is the longest day I've ever put in," Holtz said in his postgame press conference.

In the wee hours of the morning after 63–17, Whitehurst and a friend capped several hours of barhopping in Columbia with a stop at a Waffle House. The place was packed with somber, shell-shocked Gamecock fans who were wondering when they'd awaken from this awful dream. Whitehurst knew almost immediately that he wasn't going to be able to eat his breakfast in anonymity.

A cook recognized the star quarterback, announced his presence and began clapping. "I was sort of embarrassed at first," Whitehurst said. "But then the whole place started clapping and cheering. I was kind of like, 'Man, we accomplished something tonight.' It was kind of a weird moment, but kind of special. It sort of gives you chills."

Walk-on kicker Fletcher Anderson kicks the extra point—Clemson's sixty-third and final point—to close the 2003 bloodletting in Columbia. *Courtesy of Clemson University Sports Information Department.*

IN 2004, THE TYPICAL storylines in the days leading up to the Carolina-Clemson game were vastly overshadowed by questions about the sixty-seven-year-old Holtz's future. A 48–14 thumping at Florida the previous week left the Gamecocks with a 6-4 record, and the program seemed far removed from its seventeen wins in Holtz's second and third seasons.

Holtz was routinely peppered with questions about retirement, and the week before the Florida loss speculation began to percolate that Steve Spurrier would take over the Gamecocks after a failed stint with the NFL's Washington Redskins.

Two days before the Gamecocks and Tigers were to take the field, Chris Low of the *Tennessean* newspaper of Nashville unearthed a monster scoop: Spurrier, the architect of the great Florida teams that routinely spanked the Gamecocks, had agreed to replace Holtz after the season. The story became the dominant topic not just in South Carolina but also across the country. On Thursday morning, ESPN led *SportsCenter* with the development.

The news slowly became public knowledge, but the Gamecocks had learned about Holtz the previous week. He informed them of his intentions to retire prior to that thirty-four-point loss at Florida. It was a contributing factor to that result—and to what happened the following week at Clemson, according to at least one former Gamecock.

The veterans were not happy. And the young players, who committed to Holtz thinking he'd be there for the duration of their careers, were even more upset.

"The team just started to fall apart," Carolina senior center John Strickland said. "That's really where it started. We couldn't figure out why he told us then. We were 6-3. We felt like we had a chance to end the year 8-3 and get to a great bowl game, like the 2000 and 2001 teams had done. We thought we were getting it back there."

Holtz tried to rejuvenate his players by summoning several former players to deliver inspirational talks. Included was radio analyst Tommy Suggs, who reminded the team he'd beaten the Tigers three times as a Gamecocks quarterback and told them how much each one of those wins meant. Clemson had taken six of the previous seven games in the rivalry.

CLEMSON'S TEAM WAS NOT in the best of moods the week of the game. Seven days after a supposedly landmark overtime triumph at Miami, the Tigers went to Duke and lost 16–13 to a Blue Devils team whose only other victory in 2004 was over The Citadel. The tremendous finish of 2003—victories over

Florida State, Duke, South Carolina and Tennessee by a combined 156–48—did not translate to 2004, when Clemson began the year by losing four of its first five games. The Tigers carried a 5-5 record into the finale, and fans were grumbling about Bowden again as his sixth season neared its end.

Both teams were in their hotels—Carolina in Greenville, Clemson in Anderson—when the brawl flared near the end of the Pacers' game at the Pistons. Ron Artest, who played for the Pacers, sparked fights between players and fans by leaping into the stands in response to a fan having thrown a drink at him. The fight dominated the news that night, and players from both South Carolina teams watched the endless replays on television in their rooms before going to sleep.

Currie, a team captain in his senior season, remembers being completely transfixed in his hotel room with roommate Chansi Stuckey. "We were going crazy," he said. "They were fighting like they were in the streets or something. I had never seen anything like that."

The brawl was the hot topic on both teams when they gathered for their breakfasts early the next morning. It was also on the mind of Neal Brown, the police lieutenant who was preparing for the high-stress traffic situation presented by a noon game featuring the two rivals.

A nasty tone was set before kickoff, when a group of Gamecock players ventured to the bottom of the Hill to taunt the Tigers on their traditional entrance. Clemson's players weren't amused by such behavior from a team they had obliterated the year before. A bout of punching, pushing and shoving broke out in the end zone. Officials broke it up and briefly threatened to eject Currie, who ventured over from the midfield coin toss to mix it up with his counterparts.

Strickland said Gamecocks assistant Dave Roberts encouraged players to "go fight their asses" at the bottom of the Hill. "You could just tell something was going to happen," Strickland said. "Something was off that whole day."

The incident whipped Clemson's crowd into a frenzy, and the Tigers' sideline seethed. On the opening kickoff, Clemson's David Dunham shot downfield and rocked returner Cory Boyd, causing a fumble that the Tigers recovered and turned into a quick and easy touchdown.

Clemson was in control throughout, going up 14–0 in the first quarter and pulling away in the third for a 26–7 lead. In some ways, the Tigers were beating the Gamecocks worse than they did a year earlier in the 63-17 game. Players and coaches on both sidelines could feel tensions escalating as they watched a steady progression of trash talk, pushing and shoving after the whistle, and cheap shots when the refs weren't looking.

David Dunham smacks Cory Boyd on the opening kickoff to force a fumble and set the tone in the 2004 game. *Courtesy of Clemson University Sports Information Department.*

Doyle Jackson, then in his final year as an SEC referee, remembers a constant air of edginess. "We had problems before the game even started, and we thought we had them settled," he said. "But there was just a continuous bickering on the part of both teams. It was a continuous battle to try to keep people separated and keep the chatter down and prevent anything that might spark it. We were just trying to put all the fires out."

With about ten minutes on the clock and little doubt remaining with Clemson up 29–7, Jackson turned to another official. "Well," he said, "I think we can make it through this one now."

Brown wasn't as convinced. With about eight minutes to go, he left the press box and made his way to the sideline. His typical routine was to be on the field with two minutes on the clock, but he embarked early on this day. "You could just feel it tensing up," he said. "And I can remember feeling things could get bad. But I was thinking more of fans fighting in the stands or something happening on the field after the game when they let all the fans come onto the field."

WITH LESS THAN SIX minutes left and the Gamecocks facing fourth down, Syvelle Newton threw incomplete on a deep ball. Clemson defensive end Bobby Williamson wrestled Newton to the turf and gave him a small parting shot.

"I was a very emotional player and always into the game," Williamson recalls. "I kind of stood over him a little bit and taunted him. He pushed me, and me and him kind of got into it. And that was it."

Complete mayhem followed. The change of possession meant that Carolina's defense and Clemson's offense also were on the field, and fights began to pop up—here, there, everywhere.

Brown was standing to the right of Bowden on the Tigers' sideline. He tried to remain calm, tried to tell himself that the coaches and players would quickly restore order and everything would be fine:

> I remember thinking, "Good God, this ain't good." But I still didn't think it was going to be anything like it was. I'm thinking, "Throw your licks and let's get back to playing football." But then, over there was a fight. And then I look the other way and there was another one. And then the helmets were off, and they were slinging them.

That's the point when Brown turned and looked over his right shoulder, toward the student section in the southeast corner of Death Valley. The thought of fans joining the fracas sent a shudder of fear through his body:

> All those kids had their legs on the wall, ready to go. There were also kids on the Hill crowding at the bottom of the fence. It wouldn't have taken ten or twelve to come over, and then the rest of the floodgates would have opened. I couldn't help but think, "When they come over, we're not going to stop them. These players are out of control, and it's going to be the worst day of our lives trying to separate fifteen to eighteen thousand people that are rowdy and drunk." It was one of the spookiest times I've ever been on a field. It was the scaredest I've been on a field, no question about it. And the other guys will tell you they had the same feelings.

The brawl then moved toward the east end zone and was growing nastier by the moment. Holtz was in the middle of it, trying futilely to stop it. Clemson assistant Ron West suffered a hernia while trying to keep a defensive lineman on the sideline. Strickland said he remembers state troopers jawing with one another, based on their allegiances to the Tigers or Gamecocks.

Gamecocks coach Lou Holtz tries to restrain his players during the brawl that ultimately cost both teams their bowl appearances. *Courtesy of Clemson University Sports Information Department.*

Rick Stockstill, a first-year Gamecocks assistant who was on his first visit back to Death Valley after a fourteen-year stint with the Tigers, remained on the sideline with his ten-year-old son Brent. "It was out of control. It was embarrassing. It's not what that rivalry is about. It's not what college football is about. It was a sickening event. I don't take any pride in saying I was part of that game."

Most of Brown's fleet of state troopers had already left the stadium to man their posts directing postgame traffic. The few who remained intervened, an action that later drew criticism Brown never understood. "They had quit playing sports," Brown said. "As far as I'm concerned, they were fighting and attacking and were right on the verge of inciting a riot."

Thomas Hunter, who attended his first Clemson game as a weeks-old infant, was a sophomore tight end on the 2004 team. He elected to remain on the sideline, and to this day he's not sure if he made the choice from "sheer fear" or from "what my grandmother would think if she saw me trying to hit somebody on TV."

"It was something you hated to see with something that's as celebrated as the rivalry," he said. "Instead of celebrating the rivalry and the win, you're garnering bad attention for your parents, your school, your institution."

Keith "Yusef" Kelly, then a senior running back, remembers running onto the field intending to be a peacemaker. But he says his motives changed after Gamecocks offensive lineman Woodly Telfort grabbed him from behind and began choking him.

Ken Ruinard of the *Anderson Independent-Mail* snapped a photo of Kelly kicking Telfort as Telfort lay facedown on the end zone turf, protecting his helmetless head. Also in the photograph: state troopers trying to restrain Kelly.

Kelly picked up a Gamecock helmet—he suspects it was Telfort's—and paraded it around the end zone before hurling it into the student section. The photo, which was picked up by the Associated Press and stripped across the Sunday front pages of the *New York Times*, *USA Today* and the *Washington Post*, among others, made Kelly the poster child for the embarrassing incident. Kelly seemed proud of his actions when he spoke with reporters after the game: "I know die-hard Clemson fans, they are going to love it. I think I kind of left an impression. They'll have something to remember me by."

Tigers running back Yusef Kelly parades a Gamecock helmet to the delight of Clemson's student section. *Courtesy of Clemson University Sports Information Department.*

Kelly went on to a career in law enforcement, climbing high enough into the ranks to earn a position teaching entry-level officers how to keep their cool during tense situations in the field. He still believes he was miscast as a thug, largely as a result of the sensation created by the infamous photograph, but he's also convinced that the experience helped him grow up.

"There's a lot of stuff I'd definitely do differently if I could go back," he said. "It was not mature."

AFTER THE GAME, CLEMSON president James Barker exulted in the Tigers' third consecutive victory over the Gamecocks as he tailgated outside the stadium. He gave off no indication that he was alarmed over what he saw in the brawl, no hint that there would be serious ramifications from it.

The fight was a major topic the next day on ESPN, CNN and other news outlets. In addition to Kelly's antics, cameras caught Tigers running back Duane Coleman connecting on a savage punch that laid out defensive lineman Charles Silas. By late afternoon, Clemson athletics director Terry Don Phillips indicated to reporters that forfeiture of a bowl trip was in play.

On Monday—the same day that Holtz officially announced his retirement—Clemson and Carolina announced they would not attend bowls as a result of the brawl. In Columbia, players reacted to the news by stealing $18,000 worth of photos, laptops and video equipment from Williams-Brice Stadium. School president Andrew Sorensen later launched an investigation that ended in the arrests of six players.

In Clemson, Bowden had strong misgivings about the bowl ban. He was at the front of the room when Phillips announced to the team that Clemson's season was over. Bowden later said publicly that he supported the bowl ban, but privately it was a much different story.

"I wasn't big into one fail, all fail," Bowden said. "You penalize like all sports in that you penalize the ones who made the mistakes…I really wanted my team to go to a bowl game that year. I was a company guy to the media. That was my job. I know this will sound opposite of what I said at that time, but I had a pecking order to follow and I had bosses."

Williamson can count on one hand the number of times in his life he's cried. That day in the team meeting room was one of the rare moments. "I couldn't even get up out of my chair," he said. "I was bawling. I remember Coach [Brad] Scott coming up to me and trying to comfort me. We let down hundreds of thousands of fans, and we let down each other. I always took personal blame because I was one of the catalysts that started the whole ordeal."

STOCKSTILL BELIEVED THEN—AND STILL does now—that nothing would've happened without the change of possession that occurred while Williamson and Newton scuffled.

"With everybody coming onto the field, it looks like something is going on and it's a big fight," he said. "Now you've got forty-four people on the field compared to twenty-two. It turned into something that never needed to get that far. I'll go to my deathbed believing had it been on first down or second down, nothing would've ever happened."

Strickland, the Carolina offensive lineman, places the blame on Holtz for announcing his retirement to the team before the end of the regular season.

"It definitely put things into guys' minds that wouldn't have been there otherwise," he said. "I'm not a college football head coach. I don't know what it's like to be one. But I know I wish he had waited to tell us until after the Clemson game. Tell us on that Monday, when we're waiting to hear what bowl we're going to."

It's by far the worst memory Brown has in more than forty years of working the field at Clemson home games. Yet Brown cannot bring himself to conceive of how much worse it might've been had the game kicked off later in the day and been attended by fans who'd had more hours to drink and push themselves closer to the edge:

> *Noon games are horrible for traffic, horrible for TV and horrible for fans, because they don't like that when you've got a big rivalry game. But when it comes to eliminating your percentages of intoxicated people after the ballgame or during the ballgame, a noon game is a huge, huge factor.*
>
> *I personally believe they'd have come from the stands had the game been later. A twelve o'clock game saved us from a massacre that day.*

Epilogue

TURNING THE TABLES?

THIS RIVALRY, DESPITE ITS classic moments and games, is historically not a close one. Clemson cannot hear it enough. Carolina would prefer not to hear it at all.

Entering the 2011 season, though, there was a rare feeling that momentum might actually be shifting in Carolina's favor. It could not make up the stark deficit in a couple of years, or even decades, but there was some positive energy in Columbia entering the 109th edition of the game. For the first time in forty years, the Gamecocks had won consecutive games against Clemson.

"I know after last year's game, a couple of coaches and players came up to me and said, 'We're going to get your record,'" said former quarterback Tommy Suggs, referring to his three consecutive wins from 1968 to 1970. "I told them, 'You don't know how bad I'm pulling for you.' I'm sincere as I can be about that. I've had that long enough. Our team's had that long enough. We don't want to be the only championship team here, either. It's been a long time coming. It's time for somebody to get it."

To catch up on the field, first the Gamecocks had to do so off it in recruiting. Beginning with the 2009 class that included cornerback Stephon Gilmore and receiver Alshon Jeffery, Steve Spurrier and his coaching staff started to change the recruiting trend. The notable thing about those players? They're from the state of South Carolina, Gilmore from Rock Hill and Jeffery from St. Matthews. They started a trend of staying home and attending the flagship school.

Byrnes High running back Marcus Lattimore followed Gilmore and Jeffery, becoming as a freshman in 2010 the first Carolina back in a decade to rush for 1,000 yards. He broke the freshman running record set by Thomas Dendy in 1982, and his 1,197 yards were third in the school's single-season history, behind only George Rogers's seasons in 1979 and 1980. Rock Hill's Jadeveon Clowney, the consensus number one prep player in the country in the 2011 class, became the next big-splash commitment to the Gamecocks.

During Clemson's lengthy period of national prominence from the late 1970s to the early 1990s, the Tigers owned in-state recruiting. Then powers from elsewhere began invading the Palmetto State and cherry-picking its top talent. Now, the Gamecocks are luring the home-grown talent to Columbia.

"I don't think we've done enough to get back after them yet. But I'm excited, because of where we are," said Carolina's all-time leading passer, Todd Ellis, who is in his eighth season as the team's play-by-play man for radio broadcasts. "After the '80s, when I was broadcasting and doing sidelines and I'd walk down on the field, there were times when Clemson clearly had better players. That's just not the case anymore. They're very equal in terms of player size, physical skills and the coaching has been pretty even all the way. It's exciting to see us match up, personnel-wise, and let the rivalry take shape from there."

SPURRIER'S IMPACT IN THE series is still being measured, but the Ol' Ball Coach is 3-3 in the rivalry entering 2011. That's as many wins against Clemson as his predecessors Lou Holtz and Brad Scott collected in eleven combined tries.

Perspective is one thing that has perhaps helped Spurrier against Clemson. He was hired the week after the brawl in 2004. Immediately, he set out to change some things around campus. Spurrier ordered a coat of paint—or twelve—to doll up the appearance of Williams-Brice Stadium. Spurrier, the 1966 Heisman Trophy winner who built his reputation as a brash, pass-happy coach at Florida, took housekeeping into his own hands as well. He took notice of a bunch of "Beat Clemson" posters and stickers all over the walls and doors in the coaches' offices and locker room areas. "Everything was, 'Beat Clemson,' 'Beat Clemson,'" Spurrier said. "I didn't understand all that. It's a game you want to win, but why's it got to be up all over the place?"

In doing so, Spurrier put the game on level footing with every other one on the schedule. That might be blasphemous to Carolina purists, but maybe it's just what the Gamecocks needed. Maybe they had come to put too much pressure on themselves to beat Clemson. If South Carolina was competitive in the Southeastern Conference race, Spurrier figured it would also fare well in the rivalry game at the end of November.

That's easy to say now, but morale—and the belief in Spurrier, concerning Clemson *and* the SEC—was extremely low entering the 2009 game. Being demoralized 31–14 in 2008, a Carolina season that ended with three consecutive losses, did not help Spurrier's cause in dropping him to 1-3 against Clemson. Tommy Bowden had owned Lou Holtz, winning five of six, before taking two of three against Spurrier. Bowden was gone after a disastrous start to the 2008 season, and interim coach Dabo Swinney helped cement his case for the job with the resounding win over the Gamecocks in November 2008.

Bowden couldn't get the Tigers an ACC Atlantic Division title, and Swinney had that accomplishment in his back pocket entering the 2009 game in Columbia. Some wondered how seriously the Tigers would take the game given that they were playing Georgia Tech for the ACC title seven days later. The Gamecocks had lost three consecutive games, and there were growing doubts about Spurrier's ability to build the Gamecocks into a winner.

When dynamic Tigers running back C.J. Spiller returned the opening kick eighty-eight yards for a touchdown, Carolina fans sunk into despair. But what happened over the next three hours unexpectedly and dramatically reshaped the narrative. The Gamecocks controlled the rest of the game by dominating the lines of scrimmage and shutting down the Tigers' potent offense. Clemson, potentially distracted during the week by the possibility of its first ACC title since 1991, was scarcely heard from again in a 34–17 Gamecocks victory.

The 2010 game, at Death Valley, played out similarly. Clemson rolled straight down the field on its opening drive but was overwhelmed thereafter. The Tigers had no ACC title game to look forward to this time. They followed a 29–7 defeat that night with an ugly bowl loss to South Florida that ensured the school's first losing season since 1998. During a long, difficult off-season, it was hard for Clemson fans to argue against the notion that Carolina was just better. But Swinney's addition of a cutting-edge offense brought from Tulsa by first-year coordinator Chad Morris, plus the infusion of some elite freshman talent, gave the faithful hope that they could make up ground in a hurry.

To CLEMSON FANS AND former Tigers, seeing one game go into Carolina's column is one too many. They're on edge, seeing the Gamecocks succeed.

"Unfortunately for us, South Carolina has gotten better," said former Tigers linebacker Levon Kirkland, at Clemson from 1988 to 1991. "The Gamecocks now have the confidence they can beat us when they want to. Now it's up to us to kind of fight that demon. Because when you lose to a team a couple of times—and we've only lost twice in a row, but that's really unlike us—when you're that losing team you kind of wonder: 'Can we?' You start wondering if you can beat them."

Kirkland's teams never lost to the Gamecocks, by the way. The closest game was a nine-point victory in 1990. "Losing to the Gamecocks is a little different for a guy like me who's used to beating these guys on a regular basis. Even before when they beat us, you almost understood you'd beat them three or four straight times. Now they've beat us twice and you kind of wonder."

Former Clemson defensive lineman Brentson Buckner says the consecutive losses "still boil, still sting." And he speaks for every serious Tigers supporter. Clemson's board of trustees members have different backgrounds than those players, but they have a similar feeling about how things stand. It's not 1975, when the school enhanced its commitment to football following Jeff Grantz's field day, but it's not all that far off, either. Not long after last year's humbling defeat to Carolina, the administration approved plans for upgraded facilities and higher salaries for assistant coaches. The higher-ups at Clemson are getting more serious about winning, and it's not a vast stretch to think the losses to Carolina played a big role in reshaping their priorities.

As much as there might be concern on Clemson's side, at least one Carolina coach is not making assumptions that everything has changed in the rivalry based on two games.

"I don't see any disastrous problems over there or anything," said Gamecocks defensive coordinator Ellis Johnson, who also spent part of his career as a Clemson assistant.

> I'm not under any illusion that, all of a sudden, we've turned the tide on the Clemson program right now. I understand the history and how long it's been since we've won three times in a row, and all this mess. I don't get into all that. I know it reads well and writes well, but I don't think it says our program is overtaking their program. I don't think it says that. I think it says we've played well.

One fact that cannot be doubted: each win and each loss mean a lot to Carolina, Clemson and their fans. That has not changed since the rivalry began in 1896 with a 12–6 win on a rainy day at the state fair in Columbia.

Johnson returned home to Winnsboro in January 2011 for a friend's funeral. Even at that sort of somber event, Gamecocks and Tigers fans wanted to talk about Johnson's past and present loyalties. "At a funeral, at church, at a picnic…I can't go anywhere without it coming up," he said. "People are either disappointed I work here, or they're tickled to death that I work here. I mean, I'm at a funeral. It's not like I went up there to talk Carolina and Clemson. This rivalry, it's pretty damn serious to a lot of people."

Appendix

Series Records, Coaching Records and Single-Game Records

Clemson-Carolina Series Results

Clemson leads 65-39-4

1896: Carolina, 12–6
1897: Clemson, 18–6
1898: Clemson, 24–0
1899: Clemson, 34–0
1900: Clemson, 51–0
1902: Carolina, 12–6
1909: Clemson, 6–0
1910: Clemson, 24–0
1911: Clemson, 27–0
1912: Carolina, 22–7
1913: Clemson, 32–0
1914: Clemson, 29–6
1915: Tie, 0–0
1916: Clemson, 27–0
1917: Clemson, 21–13
1918: Clemson, 39–0

1919: Clemson, 19–6
1920: Carolina, 3–0
1921: Carolina, 21–0
1922: Clemson, 3–0
1923: Clemson, 7–6
1924: Carolina, 3–0
1925: Carolina, 33–0
1926: Carolina, 24–0
1927: Clemson, 20–0
1928: Clemson, 32–0
1929: Clemson, 21–14
1930: Clemson, 20–7
1931: Carolina, 21–0
1932: Carolina, 14–0
1933: Carolina, 7–0
1934: Clemson, 19–0

1935: Clemson, 44–0
1936: Clemson, 19–0
1937: Clemson, 34–6
1938: Clemson, 34–12
1939: Clemson, 27–0
1940: Clemson, 21–13
1941: Carolina, 18–14
1942: Clemson, 18–6
1943: Carolina, 33–6
1944: Clemson, 20–13
1945: Tie, 0–0
1946: Carolina, 26–14
1947: Carolina, 21–19
1948: Clemson, 13–7
1949: Carolina, 27–13
1950: Tie, 14–14
1951: Carolina, 20–0
1952: Carolina, 6–0
1953: Carolina, 14–7
1954: Carolina, 13–8
1955: Clemson, 28–14
1956: Clemson, 7–0
1957: Clemson, 13–0
1958: Carolina, 26–6
1959: Clemson, 27–0
1960: Clemson, 12–2
1961: Carolina, 21–14
1962: Clemson, 20–17
1963: Clemson, 24–20
1964: Carolina, 7–3
1965: Carolina, 17–16
1966: Clemson, 35–10
1967: Clemson, 23–12
1968: Carolina, 7–3
1969: Carolina, 27–13
1970: Carolina, 38–32
1971: Clemson, 17–7
1972: Clemson, 7–6
1973: Carolina, 32–20

1974: Clemson, 39–21
1975: Carolina, 56–20
1976: Clemson, 28–9
1977: Clemson, 31–27
1978: Clemson, 41–23
1979: Carolina, 13–9
1980: Clemson, 27–6
1981: Clemson, 29–13
1982: Clemson, 24–6
1983: Clemson, 22–13
1984: Carolina, 22–21
1985: Clemson, 24–17
1986: Tie, 21–21
1987: Carolina, 20–7
1988: Clemson, 29–10
1989: Clemson, 45–0
1990: Clemson, 24–15
1991: Clemson, 41–24
1992: Carolina, 24–13
1993: Clemson, 16–13
1994: Carolina, 33–7
1995: Clemson, 38–17
1996: Carolina, 34–31
1997: Clemson, 47–21
1998: Clemson, 28–19
1999: Clemson, 31–21
2000: Clemson, 16–14
2001: Carolina, 20–15
2002: Clemson, 27–20
2003: Clemson, 63–17
2004: Clemson, 29–7
2005: Clemson, 13–9
2006: Carolina, 31–28
2007: Clemson, 23–21
2008: Clemson, 31–14
2009: Carolina, 34–17
2010: Carolina, 29–7

In Columbia: Clemson leads 49-30-3
In Clemson: Clemson leads 16-9-1
Biggest Clemson win: 51–0 in 1900
Biggest Carolina win: 56–20 in 1975

COACHING RECORDS

Clemson Coaches v. Carolina

Walter Riggs (1896, 1899): 1-1
W.M. Williams (1897): 1-0
John Penton (1898): 1-0
John Heisman (1900–03): 1-1
Bob Williams (1906, 1909, 1913–15): 3-1-1
Frank Dobson (1910–12): 2-1
Wayne Hart (1916): 1-0
Edward Donahue (1917–20): 3-1
E.J. Stewart (1921–22): 1-1
Bud Saunders (1923–26): 1-2
Josh Cody (1927–30): 4-0
Jess Neely (1931–39): 6-3
Frank Howard (1940–69): 13-15-2
Hootie Ingram (1970–72): 2-1
Red Parker (1973–76): 2-2
Charley Pell (1977–78): 2-0
Danny Ford (1979–89): 7-3-1
Ken Hatfield (1990–93): 3-1
Tommy West (1994–98): 3-2
Tommy Bowden (1999–2008): 7-2
Dabo Swinney (2008–present): 1-2

Carolina Coaches v. Clemson

R.S. Whaley (1896): 1-0
W.P. Murphy (1897): 0-1
W. Wertenbaker (1898): 0-1
I.O. Hunt (1899–1900): 0-2

Bob Williams (1902): 1-0
Christie Benet (1909): 0-1
John Neff (1910–11): 0-2
N.B. Edgerton (1912–15): 1-2-1
Rice Warren (1916): 0-1
Dixon Foster (1917, 1919): 0-2
Frank Dobson (1918): 0-1
Sol Metzger (1920–24): 3-2
Branch Bocock (1925–26): 2-0
Harry Lightsey (1927): 0-1
Billy Laval (1928–34): 3-4
Don McCallister (1935–37): 0-3
Rex Enright (1938–42, 1946–55): 8-6-1
J.P. Moran (1943): 1-0
William Newton (1944): 0-1
Johnnie McMillan (1945): 0-0-1
Warren Giese (1956–60): 1-4
Marvin Bass (1961–65): 3-2
Paul Dietzel (1966–74): 4-5
Jim Carlen (1975–81): 2-5
Richard Bell (1982): 0-1
Joe Morrison (1983–88): 2-3-1
Sparky Woods (1989–93): 1-4
Brad Scott (1994–98): 2-3
Lou Holtz (1999–2004): 1-5
Steve Spurrier (2005–present): 3-3

SINGLE-GAME RECORDS

Individual

Most rushes: 33 by Earl Clary, Carolina, 1933
Most yards rushing: 256 by Steve Wadiak, Carolina, 1950
Most rushing touchdowns: 4 by Boo Armstrong, Clemson, 1918; 4 by Chad Jasmin, Clemson, 2003
Most pass attempts: 47 by Chris Smelley, Carolina, 2008
Most pass completions: 28 by Steve Taneyhill, Carolina, 1995; 28 by Cullen Harper, Clemson, 2007

Most passing yards: 307 by Steve Taneyhill, Carolina, 1995

Most touchdown passes: 5 by Jeff Grantz, Carolina, 1975

Most receptions: 9 by Sterling Sharpe, Carolina, 1986; 9 by Aaron Kelly, Clemson, 2007

Most receiving yards: 167 by Sterling Sharpe, Carolina, 1986

Most interception return yards: 101 by Willie Underwood, Clemson, 1980

Most tackles: 28 by Derrick Little, Carolina, 1986

Longest play: 94-yard kickoff return by Brandon Bennett/Reggie Richardson, Carolina, 1994

Longest rush: 80 yards by C.J. Spiller, Clemson, 2006

Longest pass: 81 yards, Joel Wells to Joe Pagliei, Clemson, 1954

Longest field goal: 54 yards by Scott Hagler, Carolina, 1985

Longest punt: 78 yards by Chris Gardocki, Clemson, 1990

Team

Most rushes: 72 by Carolina, 1969

Most yards rushing: 458 by Carolina, 1975

Most passing attempts: 47 by Carolina, 2008

Most passing completions: 30 by Carolina, 1995

Most passing yards: 353 by Carolina, 1995

Most touchdown passes: 5 by Carolina, 1975

Most yards total offense: 616 by Carolina, 1975

Most touchdowns: 9 by Clemson, 2003

Most points: 63 by Clemson, 2003

Most interceptions: 6 by Clemson, 1971

ABOUT THE AUTHORS

Travis Haney has covered University of Oklahoma sports for the *Oklahoman* in Oklahoma City, Oklahoma, since August 2011. He previously followed University of South Carolina sports for the *Post and Courier* for four and a half years. While in that position, he chronicled the Gamecocks' two NCAA baseball championships, writing *Gamecock Glory* in 2011 about the team's first national title. Haney also spent more than two seasons covering the Atlanta Braves for Morris News Service. Haney, thirty, has won numerous writing awards and had a 2004 feature story published in the *Best American Sports Writing* series. He lives in Norman, Oklahoma.

Larry Williams has covered Clemson football on a daily basis since 2004, when he joined the *Post and Courier* of Charleston, South Carolina. In 2008, he moved to Tigerillustrated.com, the most popular Clemson-themed site on the

Internet. From 1999 to 2003, he worked as a sportswriter at the *Augusta Chronicle* in Georgia and covered college sports at Clemson, South Carolina and Georgia. He also covered the Super Bowl, the Final Four and the Masters. In 2007, he was named South Carolina Sportswriter of the Year by the National Sportscasters and Sportswriters Association. He lives in the Clemson area with his wife and two daughters.